Month-by-Month Phonics and Vocabulary
Grade 5

by

Karen L. Loman, Amanda B. Arens,

and Patricia M. Cunningham

Carson-Dellosa Publishing Company, Inc.

Greensboro, North Carolina

This book is dedicated to the Lammers. Dave and Julia took Kaitlin to softball and soccer games, Rachel and Hannah babysat, and Claire and Jack played with her so that I could write. Thank you for being great neighbors and wonderful friends!

Karen Loman

This book is dedicated to my son Alexander McBird Arens. Alex, you bring me such happiness. Your beautiful smile and sweet charm brighten the day. I love your quirky sense of humor and am so proud of your thoughtfulness. You have always loved to read and I am thankful that it has come easily to you. Most of all, I am thankful for you. I love you so very much . . . . Mom

Amanda Arens

Credits

Editor
Joey Bland

Layout Design
Van Harris

Inside Illustrations
Lori Jackson

Cover Design
Nick Greenwood

Cover Photos
© Comstock, Inc.
© Copyright 1995 Photodisc, Inc. All Rights Reserved

ISBN 978-1-60022-413-3

Table of Contents

Table of Contents

Introduction

Big kids . . . big words! As students move into the upper grades, the words they encounter increase in size and number. These big words are harder to decode and more difficult to associate meanings with. The type of word work needed in the upper grades must focus on not only how to say big words, but how to analyze the parts of words in order to figure out their meanings. Too many students enter fifth grade thinking that reading is saying all of the words correctly. Then, students wonder why they have trouble understanding what they read.

In the following excerpt from a social studies text, there are eight words with suffixes or prefixes. Knowing how to break down the meaning of these polysyllabic words is an essential strategy for a fifth-grade student.

> The house in which representation was based on population would have the sole authority to propose tax bills. In the end, the committee presented its plan to the whole convention. The delegates soon came to understand that if they did not agree to the Great Compromise, there would be no new plan of government. (*Harcourt Horizons: United States History: Beginnings*, 2005)

In this paragraph from an upper-grade science text, morphemes are used in many ways with the same root word. Understanding how to apply meaning with the new prefixes and suffixes greatly impacts comprehension.

> Parasitoids (PAH-ruh-si-toids) are organisms that are parasitic for only one part of their life cycle. Often, parasitoids begin their lives as larvae on or in a host, living on the nutrients from the host. When the parasitoids mature, they leave their host and lead a nonparasitic life. (Brelsfoard, 2006)

The typical upper-grade student is still mastering the skills and strategies associated with being a proficient reader. Most upper-grade readers do not consistently demonstrate a mastery of higher-level thinking skills (Donahue, Daane, and Grigg, 2003). They are still developing fluency (Ivey and Broaddus, 2000), learning about word patterns—particularly within big words—and developing their vocabularies (Cunningham, 2000).

Helping students learn to read and understand polysyllabic (big) words is a critical component of the upper-grade language arts curriculum. Knowing which words to teach and finding time to teach them can be quite a challenge. This book is filled with suggestions for what to teach, how to teach, and when to teach the Working with Words Block in a fifth-grade classroom.

While this book focuses only on Working with Words, literacy instruction in an upper-grade classroom incorporates words instruction with solid reading and writing instruction. Like the Four-Blocks® Literacy Framework for primary grades, Big Blocks incorporates a balance of instructional strategies to promote the literacy development of all students. In a Big-Blocks™ classroom, time is devoted to teaching students how to comprehend text in the Guided Reading Block, how to write fluently and in a variety of genres in the Writing Block, how to read for pleasure in the Self-Selected Reading Block, and how to read, spell, and understand words and develop vocabulary in the Working with Words Block.

The Working with Words Block is multilevel because it provides instruction through the use of simple and complex words, a focus on patterns and morphemes, and a focus on transferring these words and patterns to reading and writing. Multilevel instruction focuses on the multiple learning levels and needs of all students in the class in a single lesson. A multilevel activity is so rich that students at different levels have something to learn through the same activity (Cunningham, 2004). Unlike single-level activities, multilevel activities are neither frustrating for the struggling reader and writer nor boring for those that are more advanced. When teachers provide daily, multilevel learning opportunities, more students achieve the mastery desired over time (Cunningham, Hall, and Defee, 1998). *Month-by-Month Phonics and Vocabulary: Grade 5* provides directions and complete lessons for many multilevel activities that promote the learning of morphemes, vocabulary, and spelling strategies for upper-grade readers.

If your fifth-grade students come from fourth-grade Big-Blocks classrooms, they should be familiar with the routines and procedures of the Working with Words Block. The lessons in this book are new, but the routines, procedures, and activities remain the same as those in *Month-by-Month Phonics and Vocabulary: Grade 4*. However, using the lessons in this book is not dependent on students having done the work in *Month-by-Month Phonics and Vocabulary: Grade 4*.

Effects of Morphemic Word Study

There are many reasons to devote time to word study in the upper grades:

- By fifth grade, morphological awareness is a stronger predictor of reading fluency than phonological awareness (Carlisle and Stone, 2005).

- Morphemic structure plays a part in reading Latin- and Greek-based words (Carlisle and Stone, 2005).

- Familiar base words and suffixes facilitate elementary students' reading when the morphemic structure is phonologically transparent (pronunciation of the base word remains intact) (Carlisle and Stone, 2005).

- Treiman and Cassar (1996), Bryant, Nunes, and Bindman (2000), and Rubin, Patterson, and Kantor (1991) strongly recommend that elementary school teachers provide explicit instruction in word reading and spelling that links phonological (sound), orthographic (spelling), syntactic (grammar), and morphemic elements (Carlisle and Stone, 2005).

- Morphemic structure can be used as a method of vocabulary building. Students can use morphemic structure to figure out the meanings of unfamiliar words (Carlisle and Stone, 2005).

- Students can be taught the meanings of select morphemic elements, and this morphemic knowledge enables them to infer the meanings of untaught words immediately following instruction (Baumann, Edwards, Font, Tereshinski, Kame'enui, and Olejnik, 2002).

- Morphological relationships are important to the internal lexicon (the way the brain stores and retrieves information) (Nagy, Anderson, Schommer, Scott, and Stallman, 1989).

- Morphological decomposition (taking polysyllabic words apart) is a strategy that skilled readers can be taught (Nagy, Anderson, Schommer, Scott, and Stallman, 1989).

- Knowledge of morphology plays a role in word recognition during normal reading (Nagy, Anderson, Schommer, Scott, and Stallman, 1989).

The Teacher's Guide to Big Blocks™ (Arens, Loman, Cunningham, and Hall, 2005) outlines instruction for the Big-Blocks™ Literacy Framework. Since its publication, more teachers use the multilevel Working with Words lessons and more fifth-grade students are successful in the study of words. The lessons and activities in *Month-by-Month Phonics and Vocabulary: Grade 5* are a result of feedback from teachers and observations in their classrooms. Some of the instructions and activities in this book differ from what is included in *The Teacher's Guide to Big Blocks*™. These changes reflect the authors' commitment to continuously revise activities and strategies to offer the most relevant and successful literacy instruction.

Working with Words Goals in Fifth Grade

Goal One: Teach students key words containing the major prefixes, suffixes, and spelling changes, and how to use these to decode, spell, and build meaning for many polysyllabic words. Nifty Thrifty Fifty lessons, Word Sorts, Mini-WORDO, Scavenger Hunt, Making Words, and Word Detectives help teachers and students meet this goal. Most Big-Blocks Working with Words lessons address this goal.

Goal Two: Teach students the correct spellings for high-frequency, often irregularly spelled words such as **they, friend, could, there, their, they're, right, write,** etc. Word Wall words and activities help teachers and students meet this goal.

Goal Three: Teach students that spelling rhyming words is not as easy as decoding them because some rhymes such as **right/bite, claim/name,** and **toad/code** have different spelling patterns. Writers need to develop a visual checking system and learn to use a dictionary when they are unsure about which pattern is correct. What Looks Right? lessons help teachers and students meet this goal.

Goal Four: Teach students to use cross-checking while reading and a visual checking system while writing to apply what they are learning in the Working with Words Block as they engage in meaningful reading and writing. Guess the Covered Word lessons help teachers and students meet this goal.

Introduction

Time is a perennial problem in the fifth grade. Most fifth-grade teachers try to include three 20-minute Working with Words lessons each week. A monthly schedule might look like this:

Week 1	Nifty Thrifty Fifty word introduction (Goal One)	Guess the Covered Word (Goal Four)	Word Detectives (Goal One)
Week 2	Nifty Thrifty Fifty review activity: Mini-WORDO (Goal One)	Making Words (Goal One)	Nifty Thrifty Fifty Cards (Goal One)
Week 3	Commonly misspelled words added to Word Wall (Goal Two)	Word Sort (Goal One)	What Looks Right? (Goal Three)
Week 4	Word Wall review: Riddles (Goal Two)	Scavenger Hunt (Goal One)	Nifty Thrifty Fifty Cards (Goal One)

 Note: On page 156, we have included a reproducible planning page that you can use for the Working with Words Block. On page 157, you will find a sample planning page for a month of Working with Words lessons.

Goal One: Polysyllabic Words

Morphemes are important in breaking the code of big words. Fifth-grade texts contain words that students have trouble decoding because the words are longer and have prefixes and suffixes. These texts also contain words that students have difficulty defining, particularly in content-based materials. Students need instruction in strategies that focus on building word meanings and vocabulary and using word parts, context, and morphological patterns to decode and spell big words. With the focus on big words, students will spend a majority of the Working with Words Block on morpheme study.

Decoding and spelling polysyllabic words is based on patterns, but these patterns are more sophisticated than the spelling patterns studied in the primary grades. They require that students understand how words change in their spelling, pronunciation, and meaning as suffixes and prefixes are added. For example, the **g** in **sign** seems quite illogical until you realize that **sign** is related to **signal**, **signature**, and other words containing the **sign** root. The pronunciation change from **music** to **musician** helps students understand **beauty/beautician** and **magic/magician**. Most of the lessons in this book will focus on this critical goal.

Nifty Thrifty Fifty

Words with three or more syllables follow patterns that are more sophisticated than words whose patterns consist of onsets and rimes. The patterns in these big words are morphemic units commonly referred to as roots, prefixes, and suffixes. These word features require that students understand how words change in their spelling, pronunciation, and meaning as suffixes and prefixes are added. English is the most morphologically complex of all languages. Linguists estimate that for every word a person knows, she can figure out how to decode, spell, and build meaning for six or seven other words by recognizing and using morphemic patterns in words (Nagy and Anderson, 1984). The Nifty Thrifty Fifty consists of fifty words that provide examples of the most common prefixes and suffixes, as well as common spelling changes. More than two-thirds of fifth graders have meanings for most of these words, but many upper-grade students cannot spell them (Dale and O'Rourke, 1981). Activities with the Nifty Thrifty Fifty will help students learn to use these words and the patterns in them to decode, spell, and build meanings for hundreds of other words.

The words introduced in the Nifty Thrifty Fifty are appropriate for both fourth and fifth grade. If your students worked with the Nifty Thrifty Fifty in their fourth-grade classrooms, they should be familiar with this group of words. However, students will benefit from an additional year of work with the prefixes, suffixes, and spelling changes.

The "Unpeelable" Prefixes

Many common prefixes leave independent words when they are removed. These prefixes (including **un**-, **re**-, and **under**-) are easily learned and understood by most fifth-grade students. Other common prefixes do not leave recognizable words when they are "peeled off." These prefixes (**com**-/**con**-, **em**-, **ex**-, and **per**-, etc.) add meanings to words, but you have to have a rather advanced understanding of Greek and Latin roots to see the meaning relationships. It is probably best to help students see how these are predictable spelling and pronunciation chunks rather than try to show students how to analyze these unpeelable prefixes for meaning clues.

Here are some examples of unpeelable prefixes:

Unpeelable Prefix	Meaning	Nifty Words	Other Examples
com-/con-	with or together	community/ies	competition, complain
com-/con-	with or together	composer	computer, committee
com-/con-	with or together	continuous	construction, conclusion
com-/con-	with or together	conversation	constitution, concrete
em-	to cause, to put into	employee	embassy, embryo
ex-	out or away from	expensive	excitement, explain
per-	through	performance	permanent, personality

Introduction ···

Nifty Thrifty Fifty

Word	Prefix	Meaning	Suffix	Meaning	Month Introduced
antifreeze	anti-	against			March
beautiful			-ful	full of	November
classify			-ify		November
communities*	com-	with or together	-es (y to i)	plural	November
community*	com-	with or together			November
composer*	com-	with or together	-er	someone or something that does	August/ September
continuous*	con-	with or together	-ous		December
conversation*	con-	with or together	-tion		December
deodorize	de-	reverse or take away	-ize	to make	February
different			-ent		February
discovery	dis-	opposite, against, or apart	-y		August/ September
dishonest	dis-	opposite, against, or apart			January
electricity			-ity		November
employee*	em-	to cause or put into	-ee	person who	February
encouragement*	en-	to cause or put into	-ment		August/ September
expensive*	ex-	out or away from	-ive		October
forecast	fore-	before or in front of			March
forgotten			-en (double t)		December
governor			-or	someone who does	October
happiness			-ness		November
hopeless			-less	without	August/ September
illegal*	il-	opposite			January
impossible*	im-	opposite			August/ September

* indicates an unpeelable prefix

Word	Prefix	Meaning	Suffix	Meaning	Month Introduced
impression*	im-	in, into, toward, or within	-ion		October
independence*	in-	opposite	-ence		October
international	inter-	between, or across	-al		February
invasion*	in-	in	-sion		February
irresponsible*	ir-	opposite	-ible	able to, inclined to	January
midnight	mid-	middle, halfway			March
misunderstand	mis-	opposite or wrong			January
musician			-ian		August/ September
nonliving	non-	not	-ing (drop e)		December
overpower	over-	more than, too much			March
performance*	per-	through	-ance		January
prehistoric	pre-	before	-ic		February
prettier			-er (y to i)	more	November
rearrange	re-	back or again			January
replacement	re-	back or again	-ment		January
richest			-est	the most	August/ September
semifinal	semi-	half or partly			March
signature			-ture		Febuary
submarine	sub-	under or below			October
supermarkets	super-	higher or bigger	-s	plural	March
swimming			-ing		December
transportation	trans-	across or through	-tion		October
underweight	under-	below or less than			March
unfinished	un-	opposite	-ed	past tense	October
unfriendly	un-	opposite	-ly		August/ September
unpleasant	un-	opposite	-ant (drop e)		December
valuable			-able	able to, inclined to	December

* indicates an unpeelable prefix

Introduction ···

Introducing Nifty Thrifty Fifty Words

As a rule, fifth-grade teachers find that they are most successful when they gradually introduce the Nifty Thrifty Fifty words over the course of the school year. Teachers generally introduce seven to eight Nifty Thrifty Fifty words each month. The words are introduced in the first week of the month to give plenty of time for practice and review. Students will do extensive work with these words until their spelling and decoding becomes automatic. Students also see and practice many other words that can be decoded and spelled using the patterns from the Nifty Thrifty Fifty words. Suggestions for Nifty Thrifty Fifty words and other words that can be made from the prefixes, roots, and suffixes can be found in each monthly section of this book.

Because there are so many words that can be made and spelled using the various roots, prefixes, and suffixes in the 50 words, we encourage both fourth- and fifth-grade teachers to teach the Nifty Thrifty Fifty lessons. Fifth-grade teachers will see students extend the use of the morphemic word parts as they become more familiar and confident with these complex patterns.

Reviewing Nifty Thrifty Fifty Words

Throughout each month of the school year, have students chant and write the Nifty Thrifty Fifty words as practice. As students are cheering and writing the spelling of each word, ask them to identify the root, prefix, and suffix. Ask them to talk about how the prefix and suffix affect the meaning of the root word. When you have a few extra minutes during the week, have students review the Nifty Thrifty Fifty words with an enjoyable riddle or game. The activities that will help your students review the Nifty Thrifty Fifty words are Riddles (page 23), Mini-WORDO (page 37), and Be a Mind Reader (page 52).

Beyond Nifty Thrifty Fifty
Nifty Thrifty Fifty Cards

Once students can automatically, quickly, and correctly spell the new Nifty Thrifty Fifty words and explain how they are composed, help them see how these words can assist them in decoding and spelling other words. Have students spell words that are found in the new words. Next, tell students that they can combine parts of the new words to spell other words. In addition to making familiar words, students will make neologisms.

A **neologism** is a made-up word that consists of common prefixes, roots, and suffixes, but doesn't currently exist as a real word. For example, an aerobics instructor told her class that each of them was working on the gluteus maximus to turn it into a gluteus minimus! Neologisms allow students to use what they are learning about morphemes to create fun and interesting new words.

To help students spell new words, this book includes monthly index card activities that were introduced in *The Teacher's Guide to Big Blocks*™ (Arens, Loman, Cunningham, and Hall, 2005). See page 24 for more information on Nifty Thrifty Fifty Cards.

Word Sorts

To extend the Nifty Thrifty Fifty, students will do Word Sorts to learn a selection of words with a variety of morphemic connections. Each Word Sort will focus on one of the prefixes, suffixes, or spelling changes learned in a previously introduced Nifty Thrifty Fifty word. Word sorts help students connect the morphemes learned in the Nifty Thrifty Fifty to words that occur in their independent reading and in their content-area studies. See page 39 for more information and directions for Word Sorts.

Root Word Lessons

Word lessons that focus on root words allow students to see how knowing the root of one word can help them find the meaning of a new word. The lessons included in this book are based on root words that have many recognizable words associated with them. Students enjoy seeing how many words they can read and write from just one root. See page 42 for more information on Root Word lessons.

Scavenger Hunt

Scavenger Hunt is an activity that follows the introduction and practice of important prefixes, suffixes, and spelling changes in the Nifty Thrifty Fifty words. Students need to see the use and value of the 50 words and their word parts beyond simply memorizing them. Sometime during the month, have students do a Scavenger Hunt while reading texts to find all of the words that have an identified prefix, suffix, or spelling change represented by the Nifty Thrifty Fifty words introduced that month. Students will chart their findings during the week. At the end of the week, you will guide students in analyzing each word. See page 42 for more information on Scavenger Hunt.

Making Words

Making Words is an active, hands-on, manipulative activity in which students learn how adding letters and moving letters around creates new words (Cunningham, 2000). Making Words lessons highlight patterns and demonstrate how changing one letter changes the whole word. Each lesson ends with students using patterns to sort the words they made and transferring those patterns to decode or spell other words. Be sure that you include the sort and transfer portions of the lesson. They are critical, so don't overlook them when planning for time and strategy instruction. For fifth-grade lessons, it is important to include words with common roots so that students can also sort for prefixes, suffixes, and spelling changes. You may also want to select lessons with a secret word that is either a vocabulary word from a current content-area lesson or a word that is a combination of the morphemes from the Nifty Thrifty Fifty. See page 25 for more information on Making Words. Suggestions for Making Words lessons are included in each monthly section of this book.

Word Detectives

Word Detectives (Cunningham, 2000) is an activity that encourages students to answer the questions:

Do I know any other words that look and sound like this word?

Are any of these look-alike/sound-alike words related to each other?

The answer to the first question should help students with pronouncing and spelling the word. The answer to the second question should help students discover what, if any, meaning relationships

Introduction ···

exist between this new word and other words in their meaning vocabularies. These lessons are particularly well-suited for content-based vocabulary instruction. See page 28 for more information on Word Detectives.

Homework Suggestions

In addition to the activities that focus on morphemes, there are also homework suggestions. Directions for homework assignments may be found in each set of monthly plans.

Goal Two: Word Wall

It is estimated that a little over 100 words make up 50 percent of what people read and write (Fry, Fountoukidis, and Polk, 1985). Many of these high-frequency words have irregular spellings. These words are often introduced and assessed as spelling words in the primary grades, and it is assumed that students know them before they advance to the upper grades. Many fifth-grade teachers express concern that students spell **they** as **thay** or **was** as **wuz** in their daily writing. Students also continue to confuse **there**, **their**, and **they're**, as well as other common homophones. If you give students a list of words to memorize and spell for a Friday spelling test, they generally do well on the test, but continue to misspell those same words in their daily writing. The following fourth- and fifth-grade rough-draft writing samples show many of these mistakes.

Student Sample #1:

I thought it was a neat givt to get for my birthday and I thanked my mom and my dad, sisster, brother and my uncle for a very great Birthday I had with the hole family there to be able to selabrate with. I couldn't of done without my family.

Student Sample #2:

I was in Minnesota and I cold my brother and asked if he could come over sometime. So he siad yes.

Student Sample #3:

While we were there I playd with ther dog dolly. And I opend presents. Then I recived a gift card from my uncle.

Student Sample #4:

I just wanted to say thank you very much it was fun. I hope we see you agian soon. I apreateated it very much.

These are not students who are lazy, low achievers, or ignoring what they have learned. These students have written these words incorrectly so many times that they have committed the misspellings to memory. In fact, the human brain has the remarkable ability to make actions "automatic" after having processed them several times. Once something is put into the automatic part of the brain, it is carried out without any conscious thought.

This automatic function of the brain is a wonderful asset when it stores things automatically in their correct forms. Once a person has lots of practice driving, he can shift, use turn signals, and steer while talking to passengers, listening to the radio, planning dinner, or talking on the phone. The brain can do many automatic things at the same time, but only one nonautomatic thing at a time. When children are just beginning to write, they spell words the logical or phonetic way—**thay** (they), **sed** (said), and **frend** (friend). Because these are high-frequency words, students write them many times. Each time they write these words, they spell them logically, but incorrectly. After a certain number of times (it varies from brain to brain), the brain assumes that these are the correct spellings and puts them into its automatic compartment! Later, the child learns the correct spellings for **they**, **said**, and **friend** as part of a spelling list, but they are only practiced one week for the test. Students don't get enough practice for their brains to replace the incorrect spellings in their automatic compartments. When a person is writing, the brain's nonautomatic function is focused on meaning, and, except for an occasional new word, the brain's automatic compartment takes care of spelling. When the words in the automatic compartment are spelled correctly, this is a marvelous function of the brain. But, when the words in the automatic compartment are spelled incorrectly, it changes "Practice makes perfect," to "*Perfect* practice makes perfect."

The focus of Word Wall activities is to put the correct spelling of words into the automatic compartments of students' brains. This won't be a quick fix. Students may need to practice the words for several years before their brains accept the required changes.

Selecting Word Wall Words

Look at your students' first-draft writing to determine which words most students need to learn or relearn. A list of suggested words, categorized by priority, is provided in this book.

- **First Priority:** High-Frequency, Commonly Misspelled Words (page 126)

- **Second Priority:** Common Contractions and Compounds, including words that are not compounds but students write them as compounds (page 128)

- **Third Priority:** Common Homophones (page 128)

- **Fourth Priority:** Spelling Change Examples—doubling letters, dropping **e**, changing **y** to **i** (page 129)

- **Fifth Priority**: Other Homophones (page 129)

- **Sixth Priority:** Less Common Homophones; Other Commonly Misspelled Words (page 129)

Compare the errors in your students' writing with the prioritized lists. We recommend that you identify, practice, and post only 80–100 words from the lists. With the addition of the Nifty Thrifty Fifty words, there will be 130–150 words on your Word Wall by the end of the year. Once a word has been added to the Word Wall, hold students accountable for spelling the word correctly in all of their writing. Once a word with a spelling change, prefix, root, or suffix has been added to the Word Wall, coach and encourage students to use those changes and patterns with other words in their daily writing.

Introduction ···

Because old habits are hard to break, only 8–10 "new" Word Wall words should be introduced and placed on the wall each month. Display the words, arranged by first letter, somewhere in the classroom. The words need to be big and bold so that students can easily see them from any place in the room.

In addition to the classroom display, you may give each student a "portable" Word Wall to keep at her desk or to take home. Since the rule is that Word Wall words must be spelled correctly in all writing—including homework—a portable Word Wall is very helpful.

Introducing Word Wall Words

New Word Wall words are usually introduced a couple of weeks after the introduction of new Nifty Thrifty Fifty words. In a 20-minute lesson, you will explain to students what makes the selected words difficult to spell, ask them to chant the words, and have them print each word one time. It is preferable that the writing occurs in the context of the initial introduction. This means that all modes of instruction are employed to teach the new words: visual (looking at the posted words), auditory (chanting), and kinesthetic (writing).

Some of the words you introduce will have spelling changes. It will be helpful to underline or highlight the spelling changes on the posted words so that students can transfer that information to other words they read and spell.

Reviewing Word Wall Words

To assist the brain in "rewiring" the incorrectly learned words, you and students will practice the words in a variety of ways. When there are a few minutes of available time, have students practice the words by chanting and writing them. You may choose to review the words with Word Wall Riddles (page 32) or Be a Mind Reader (page 52).

Making Word Wall Words Automatic

When you see a Word Wall word misspelled in any student's writing, write **WW** on the word. The student must write the correct spelling of the word and return the paper to you. Students don't like being given back their papers to fix errors. After several times for the same word, a student will write it correctly or fix it before he turns it in. Without this level of accountability, many students won't take the Word Wall seriously; nor will they believe that you expect them to spell the words correctly every single time! Consequently, students won't relearn the words they write most often.

Goal Three: Visual Checking System

In English, words that have the same spelling pattern usually rhyme. The complication is that some rhymes have multiple spelling patterns, such as **plight** and **trite**. This is not a problem when students are trying to read unfamiliar words, but it is a big problem when students attempt to spell unfamiliar words. A good writer generally writes a word the way she thinks it should be spelled, then decides if the word "looks right." If it does, the good writer continues to write. If it doesn't, the good writer checks her spelling in a dictionary. What Looks Right? lessons help students use these important self-monitoring strategies. See page 33 for more information on What Looks Right? lessons.

Goal Four: Cross-Checking

Good readers use multiple cues to figure out unknown words in text. They simultaneously cross-check for meaning, structure (grammar), and visual information (letters and sounds). Guess the Covered Word is a guided activity that has students cross-check meaning (including structure), word length, and all of the beginning letters up to the vowel (onset) to figure out words in a game-like fashion. You may develop lessons using content texts or literature selections. There are suggestions and sample lessons in each monthly section, but those are just to give you ideas. The best lessons will be derived from your own content and literature selections. See page 34 for more information on Guess the Covered Word.

Struggling Readers

Month-by-Month Phonics for Upper Grades (Cunningham and Hall, 1998) is a book designed for struggling readers. Some of the activities in this book (Word Wall, Nifty Thrifty Fifty, Making Words, and Guess the Covered Word) come from that resource. However, the examples provided in this book go beyond the lessons provided in *Month-by-Month Phonics for Upper Grades*. Here are some ways other teachers have supported struggling readers who need decoding and spelling help.

Most of Class Below Third-Grade Reading Level

If the majority of your class functions below a third-grade reading level, use the Four-Blocks® Literacy Model. That means 30 minutes of Working with Words instruction every day. The types of activities you will do with students differ and could come from *Month-by-Month Phonics for Upper Grades*.

Students Still Spell Letter by Letter

For students who still spell letter by letter, there are several activities that will help them focus on patterns. *Reading/Writing Simple Rhymes* (Cunningham and Hall, 2005) gives students practice with using spelling patterns to decode and spell hundreds of words. *Systematic Sequential Phonics They Use* (Cunningham, 2000) helps readers of any age learn phonics through Word Wall and Making Words activities.

The *Systematic Sequential Phonics* lessons are available in a computer program called *Word Maker* (Don Johnston, Inc.). Brand Name Phonics, an activity included in *Month-by-Month Phonics for Upper Grades*, helps students focus on common spelling patterns using familiar product names such as Pop-Tarts®, Crest®, and Coke®.

Introduction

Students with Some Spelling/Decoding Skills but Struggling

In addition to the lessons offered in *Month-by-Month Phonics for Upper Grades*, there are other professional resources you will find helpful. *Prefixes and Suffixes: Systematic Sequential Phonics and Spelling* (Cunningham, 2002) includes Word Wall and Making Words lessons that focus on the most common morphemes. *Reading/Writing Complex Rhymes* (Cunningham and Hall, 2005) focuses on multiple ways to spell the same rhyme (for example, **ale** and **ail**) and connects to the What Looks Right? lessons students will be doing.

For struggling readers, as with all students, it is critical that each word activity end with a transfer step. The two questions that lead to transfer are:

> How will doing this make you a better reader?

> How will doing this make you a better writer?

Many struggling students have been given additional skills instruction, but they lack the knowledge to see how skills connect to the reading and writing they are trying to do. It is essential that the person providing this additional instruction assists students in making the transfer back to real reading and writing when they do word work.

Instruction for struggling readers happens in addition to the instruction that is provided to the whole class. The best way to support struggling readers with their phonics work is to give them a double dose of instruction. You, a resource teacher, a paraprofessional, or a volunteer, may offer additional instruction.

If you are working with students who have never been in a Four-Blocks classroom and have very little experience with Working with Words routines, you may need to alter the amount and type of phonics/Working with Words instruction that you provide within the context of Big Blocks. The lessons and strategies in *Month-by-Month Phonics for Upper Grades* are also appropriate for students with little word work experience.

Challenges to Working with Words

- **Many fifth-grade teachers begin to look for ways to save time and may consider instruction in words to be important only for younger students.**
  The type of words instruction you provide is important to consider. Older students also need instruction in morphemes. Spending only 60 minutes per week on words will have a great effect on students' ability to read and write well.

- **Your own morpheme knowledge may be a challenge to instruction. If this is an area where you feel uncomfortable, you may be tempted to avoid the instruction altogether.**
  Instead of avoiding instruction in morphemes, use this book and the many other listed resources to grow your own knowledge along with your students'. See page 159 for professional resources to assist you in growing that knowledge.

- **Students aren't making the level of transfer you would like to see.**
  The two questions we typically ask teachers who we work with are, "Do you chant and write those words on a regular basis?" and "Do you hold students accountable for the spelling of those words in all of the writing they do?" It can be a challenge to force yourself to chant with students. You may feel foolish, or your students may resist. However, the lack of a rhythmic connection may contribute to the lack of transfer. And, telling students that they must spell the Word Wall words and Nifty Thrifty Fifty words correctly, but not holding them accountable in any way, will not convey the importance of these words to students. To make the most of the Working with Words Block, find the time, complete all of the parts, and increase your own word knowledge.

Working with Words: Connections to Other Blocks

Each of the Big Blocks connects and intersects with the other Blocks to assist students in transferring their learning from one Block to another. Here are a few ways that the Working with Words Block connects to the other Blocks and some ways you can help students transfer their learning about words to their reading and writing.

Working with Words: Connections to Guided Reading

Students will read many materials that have big words, particularly Guided Reading materials with content connections.

- Help students identify when to use prefixes and suffixes to read new words or create meaning for new words.

- Have students use Guided Reading materials to find words for the Scavenger Hunt (page 42).

Working with Words: Connections to Writing

As students' reading vocabularies increase, so should their writing vocabularies. At the same time, the common words students use need to be spelled correctly.

- Hold students accountable for always spelling posted words (Word Wall and Nifty Thrifty Fifty words) correctly.

- Encourage and support students as they use the prefixes, suffixes, and spelling changes that you introduce.

Working with Words: Connections to Self-Selected Reading

Students need to transfer what they learn about words to their personal reading.

- Review decoding strategies during Self-Selected Reading mini-lessons on days when you don't have a phonics/spelling lesson.

- Have students keep track of words they find that are hard to decode and/or have unfamiliar meanings that they have figured out. These words can be recorded in their Big-Blocks Notebooks or on sticky notes.

Introduction

Note: For more information on Big-Blocks Notebooks and other Big-Blocks ideas, see *The Teacher's Guide to Big Blocks*™ (Arens, Loman, Cunningham, and Hall, 2005).

- Occasionally, have students keep track of words they read during Self-Selected Reading that have prefixes, suffixes, or spelling changes that match what has been studied. Be cautious! Focusing too much on words may detract from students' attention to meaning.

- Occasionally, have students share "sticky note/notebook" words in Self-Selected Reading conferences.

A Final Word on Phonics Instruction

In a summary of research on phonics instruction, Stahl, Duffy-Hester, and Stahl (1998) summarized that good phonics instruction:

- should not teach rules, need not use worksheets, should not dominate instruction, and does not have to be boring.

- should provide sufficient practice in reading words—reading words in isolation, reading words in stories, and writing words.

- should lead to automatic word recognition.

- is only one part of reading instruction.

Month-by-Month Phonics and Vocabulary: Grade 5 builds on these basic principles and expands on them to incorporate instruction in morphological patterns. This instruction will equip fifth-grade students to read, understand, and spell complex words.

August/September

Month at a Glance

It is late August/early September in your fifth-grade classroom. The first few weeks of school are all about establishing routines and structure. Students will be studying words—big words and high-frequency words. Look at the first drafts your students are writing to see which commonly misspelled words need to be on the Word Wall. Choose 8–10 frequently used and frequently misspelled words to begin your Word Wall.

The activities in this book have been used successfully with fifth-grade students in the Working with Words Block. Working with Words activities are important, but without real reading and writing, students will not have sufficient exposure to words in a reading/writing context to become proficient with the patterns and morphemes they will be studying.

Here are the major things you will do during Working with Words in August/September to help move students toward meeting all four goals:

- **Goal One:** Polysyllabic Words

  Add eight Nifty Thrifty Fifty words to the Word Wall. Use riddles to review the words. Have students use the Nifty Thrifty Fifty Cards to explore combinations of prefixes, suffixes, and root words. Use the Making Words lesson to focus on the prefix -**en** and the root word **courage**. Use the Word Detectives lessons to help students use the prefixes and suffixes of content-area words to determine meanings.

- **Goal Two:** Word Wall Words

  Add 8–10 words that are commonly misspelled in your students' writing to the Word Wall. Use spare minutes to review and practice all of the words through chanting, writing, and Word Wall Riddles.

- **Goal Three:** Visual Checking

  Use the What Looks Right? lesson to focus on the **ear** and **eer** patterns.

- **Goal Four:** Cross-Checking

  Use Guess the Covered Word lessons to introduce content-area vocabulary or highlight a part of speech. Most importantly, Guess the Covered Word provides the opportunity to teach a valuable reading strategy. This month, you might consider choosing excerpts from social studies texts.

Goal One: Polysyllabic Words

By fifth grade, morphological awareness is a stronger predictor of reading success than phonological awareness (Carlisle and Stone, 2005). In Big-Blocks™ classrooms, students will spend most of the Working with Words Block working with polysyllabic words.

Nifty Thrifty Fifty Words

The Nifty Thrifty Fifty words that have been selected for each month will require students to focus on important morphemes. Students will practice and review the morphemes in the Nifty Thrifty Fifty words and find other words with morphemes in their daily reading.

Introducing Nifty Thrifty Fifty Words

1. Analyze each word. Talk about meaning; determine the root, prefix, and suffix; and note any spelling changes. These explanations are provided in each monthly section.

2. Have students practice the new Nifty Thrifty Fifty words by saying the letters in each word aloud in a rhythmic, chanting fashion. Fifth-grade students (and teachers) may be reluctant to chant the words because it seems rather "elementary." However, the chanting may be nothing more than saying each letter in a rhythmic way. It may involve clapping, tapping a pencil or foot, or doing a different activity for the prefix, root, and suffix. Be as creative as you and your students are willing to be.

3. Finally, have students write each word one time. Be sure that they pay attention to the letters and the sequence of letters. Don't ask students to write each word five times. They will do this "mechanically" without focusing on the individual letters. The words should also be printed in manuscript, not written in cursive. Words to be committed to memory for later use should always be printed for easier recall.

   This is a 20-minute lesson. If time allows, it is preferable that the writing occur in the context of the initial introduction. This means that all modes of instruction are employed to teach the new word: visual (looking at the posted word), auditory (chanting), and kinesthetic (writing). It also means that you will need to keep a fairly brisk pace so that students don't get bored and you don't spend more time on this activity than you have or need.

4. Check the words by having students say them again in a rhythmic chant, touching each letter as they say it.

5. Post the words on the Word Wall under the beginning letter of the word.

---

composer: A composer is a person who composes something. The prefix **com-** means "with or together." The root word **pose** means "put." The suffix -**er** can mean "a person or thing that does something" such as a writer, teacher, or reporter. When -**er** is added to a word that ends in **e**, the original **e** is dropped before the suffix is added.

discovery: Discovery is the root word **cover** with the prefix **dis-** and the suffix -**y**. The root word **cover** can mean "to hide something." The prefix **dis-** often changes a word to an opposite form. It can also mean "apart." Therefore, when you discover something, it is no longer hidden. Other words where **dis-** means the opposite include **disappear**, **disagree**, and **dishonest**. Other words ending with -**y** include **robbery**, **victory**, **bakery**, and **pottery**.

encouragement: The root word for encouragement is **courage**. So, encouragement is made from the prefix **en-** (which means "in or make"), the root word **courage**, and the suffix -**ment**. In this word, -**ment** means the action of encouraging. Other words where **en-** means "in or make" include **endear**, **enclose**, and **endanger**. Other words with -**ment** include **development**, **amusement**, and **government**.

hopeless: Students should easily see the root word **hope** and the suffix -**less**. The suffix -**less** means "without." Similar words are **painless**, **homeless**, and **joyless**. There are no spelling changes.

impossible: This is the root word **possible** with the prefix **im-**. In this and in many other words, including **impatient** and **immature**, the prefix **im-** changes the word to an opposite.

musician: This is the root word **music** with the suffix -**ian**. The suffix -**ian** can indicate a person who does something. A musician is a person who makes music. A **beautician** helps make you **beautiful**. There is no spelling change, but the pronunciation changes. Have students say the words **music** and **musician**, as well as **magic** and **magician**. Ask them to notice how the pronunciations change.

richest: Students should recognize the root word **rich** and the suffix -**est**, which means "the most." Other examples of -**est** words include **shortest**, **craziest**, **smartest**, and **biggest**.

unfriendly: The prefix **un-** often changes a word to its opposite meaning, such as in **unnecessary** and **unhappy**. The suffix -**ly** means "resembling" and changes **friend** to **friendly** (noun to adjective). Other -**ly** words that change a noun into an adjective include **fatherly** and **scholarly**.

Nifty Thrifty Fifty Review Activities

Nifty Thrifty Fifty Riddles

Students often enjoy reviewing the Nifty Thrifty Fifty words through riddles. You can help them do this by giving them clues to the word(s) you want them to write. Have each student number a piece of paper from 1–8 (or the number of words you have time to review).

Give the following clues for the new Nifty Thrifty Fifty words introduced this month:

1. Write the two-syllable word with a suffix that means "without." (hopeless)
2. Write the word that has the root word **cover**. (discovery)
3. Write the word with only a prefix. (impossible)
4. Write the only word with a spelling change. (composer)
5. Write the word with a suffix that changes the pronunciation of the root word. (musician)
6. Write the four-syllable word with the prefix **en-** and a suffix. (encouragement)
7. Write the word with a suffix that means "the most." (richest)
8. Write the word with a prefix that means "opposite" and the root word **friend**. (unfriendly)

Have each student check her own paper by chanting the letters aloud once more, and underlining each letter as she says it.

Beyond Nifty Thrifty Fifty

Nifty Thrifty Fifty Cards

We recommend the following sequence of activities to help students spell and define words using the morphemes written on the Nifty Thrifty Fifty Cards:

1. Have students write each of the prefixes, roots, and suffixes introduced this month on individual cards. Use three colors of cards—one for prefixes, one for root words, and one for suffixes. (You may use index cards, pieces of colorful card stock, or other heavy paper.) If a word has additional letters that assist in spelling and/or pronunciation, have students write those letters on separate cards that are a fourth color. Have students write the word parts on cards as a part of the introduction of the new words, when they have a few extra minutes during the week, or as homework.

2. Guide students in making new words using prefixes, roots, and suffixes by telling them the words to build. While students are building each word, use it in a sentence. For example, you might ask students to combine the word parts from **unfinished**, **independence**, and **valuable** to make **undependable**. ("We can't count on him to bring dinner because he is **undependable**.")

3. After students make the words you suggest, ask them to make new words on their own. Ask students to share their words with partners, or if time allows, have a few students share their words with the whole class.

4. Next, explain to students that they are going to make neologisms. A neologism is a new word that is made of common prefixes, roots, and suffixes. A neologism doesn't currently exist as a real word, but it makes sense. For example, **colorize** is a word now, but it was a neologism until filmmakers needed a word to describe what they were doing to old black-and-white films. Other neologisms that have come into use because of technology are **texting**, **blogger**, and **Internet**.

5. Give students a neologism to make or to define. We recommend providing a riddle or saying a sentence that includes the neologism to help students build meaning. For example, you might tell students to think of a word that answers the riddle, "What word means to take away something's beauty?" (debeautyize)

6. After making the neologism you suggest, ask each student to make a new neologism on her own using the morphemes introduced through the Nifty Thrifty Fifty. Have students make up riddles or say sentences that will help others know how to define and spell their neologisms. Ask students to share their neologisms with partners, or if time allows, have a few students share their neologisms with the whole class.

For this month's lesson, students should put the following morphemes on cards:

prefix	root	suffix
com-	pose	-er
en-	courage	-ment
	hope	-less
dis-	cover	-y
un-	friend	-ly
	rich	-est
	music	-ian
im-	possible	

Students will keep these cards all year. You may choose to have them store their cards in resealable plastic bags.

Words to make: hopelessly, discourage

Ask students to make their own real words from the morphemes.

Neologism to make: uncoverly

Ask a student to use the word in a sensible sentence. Be sure the sentence defines the word as "something that can't be covered." For example, "A lit candle is uncoverly."

Ask students to make their own neologisms. Suggest that they make up riddles or say sentences that will help other students discover the spelling and meaning of their neologisms.

Nifty Thrifty Fifty Cards Homework
Give each student a copy of the August/September Morpheme Chart (page 134). Each student should work at home to create two additional words by combining prefixes, root words, and suffixes from the chart. Then, he should also try to create one more neologism. Each student should write a riddle or defining sentence that reflects the meaning of the newly created word.

Making Words
Making Words is an active, hands-on, manipulative activity in which students learn how adding letters and moving letters around creates new words. Each lesson is planned by selecting a "secret" word—a word which can be made from all of the letters given. For older students, the best secret words are either related to content or contain familiar morphemes. Once the secret word is chosen, students will make 10–15 words using the same letters. Students will make some easy words, some harder words, some rhyming words, and some related words, starting with short words and building to longer words. Prior to the lesson, you will need to write or type the words students will make.

Hint: If you choose to type the word cards, consider using a 125 or 150 point font.

To begin the Making Words lesson, give each student a copy of the letter strip for that month (pages 150–152) and have her cut or tear the letters apart. Have students write the matching capital letter on the back of each letter. Place larger letter cards with the same letters in a pocket chart, or use clear letter tiles on an overhead projector.

Hint: You can make clear letter tiles by cutting a sheet of transparency film into small squares, then writing the letters for the lesson on the squares. The letters should be arranged in alphabetical order with the vowels first, then the consonants.

Make Words: As the lesson begins, the letter cards are visible at the front of the room and students have the same letters at their desks. Guide students to make the words by saying, "Take five letters (or whatever the correct number is) and spell _____." Then, use the word in a sentence. Use this same process for each word students will make. For the last word—the "secret" word—encourage students to figure out what word can be made from all of the letters. If students have difficulty, try giving hints such as "This word is related to the word _____."

Assign one student to be the letter manipulator. As students make each word at their desks, the letter manipulator makes the word with the letters in the pocket chart or on the overhead. When a student figures out the secret word, let that student spell it aloud for the letter manipulator. Finally, tell students the secret word and ask them all to make it.

Once students have made the word, place the word card in the pocket chart or on the board so that everyone can see it.

Sort: When all of the words have been made, lead students in sorting the word cards into columns for rhyming patterns, prefixes, roots, suffixes, and spelling changes.

Transfer: For the last part of the lesson, have students use the sorted rhyming patterns to read and spell other words. This part of the lesson is critical, so don't overlook it! Write two or three words that use the identified patterns on index cards. Say to students, "Pretend you are reading and come to a new word." Show them a word with a rhyme that they just sorted for. Tell students not to say the word aloud but to read it silently to themselves. Show everyone the transfer word. Have a student place the transfer word in the correct column. Ask students to use the pattern to decode the new word. Now, have a student pronounce the word. Have students pretend they are reading another new word. Show students the next word and have a student place it in the correct column before reading it aloud.

After reading two words, tell students to pretend they are writing and need to spell a word. Say a word they might use in their writing. Tell students not to say the letters in the word aloud until you ask someone to spell it. Ask a student to tell how the word begins. Then, have the student find and use the appropriate rhyme to spell the word. After the student spells the word aloud, show it on a card and have a student place it in the correct column. Do this again with another word.

End the lesson by asking students how Making Words makes them better readers and how Making Words makes them better writers. Remind students that they can use prefixes, suffixes, and rhymes to help them read and spell words in their daily reading and writing.

encourage

Letters: a e e o u c g n r

Make Words: age, ace, nag, rag, rage, cage, race, once, ounce, eager, orange, enrage, courage, encourage

Directions:

- Tell students how many letters to use to make each word.
- Emphasize how changing just one letter or rearranging letters makes a different word.

  "Add a letter to **rag** to spell **rage**."

  "Change one letter in **rage** to spell **cage**."

- When students are not just adding or changing one letter, cue them to start over.

  "Start over and use six letters to spell **orange**."

- Give meaning or sentence clues when needed to clarify the word they are making.

  "Start over and use six letters to spell **enrage**. 'When you **enrage** someone, you make them very, very angry.'"

- Give students one minute to figure out the secret word, then give clues if needed.

  "Our secret word is related to the word **courage**."

Sort: Sort related words and use sentence clues to show how they are related.

rage, enrage

"When the thief discovered that the stolen money was missing, he flew into a **rage**. He was **enraged**."

courage, encourage

"When you **encourage** someone, you try to give him **courage**."

Sort rhymes:

ace	age
race	rage
	cage
	enrage

Reading Transfer: disgrace, backstage

Tell students, "Pretend you are reading and come to a new word." Have students put the words under the appropriate rhymes and use the rhymes to decode them.

Spelling Transfer: retrace, outrage

Tell students, "Pretend you are writing and need to spell each of these words." Have students tell you how each word begins. Then, have students find and use the appropriate rhymes to finish spelling each new word.

Making Words Homework

A Making Words Homework reproducible is available on page 153. Send home the letters for **encourage** with students for them to make and remake words. Tell them that their Making Words homework has two parts. First, they should make as many words as they can remember from class. Second, they should make any new words they can think of with the letters in **encourage**.

Word Detectives

Word Detectives is an activity that encourages students to answer the questions:

Do I know any other words that look and sound like this word?

Are any of these look-alike/sound-alike words related to each other?

Word Detectives lessons are particularly well-suited for content-based vocabulary instruction. These words should be polysyllabic with morphemes so that students can practice taking them apart to make meaning.

Explain that words, like people, sometimes look and sound alike but are not related. If this is the first time you use this analogy, you will want to spend some time talking about people with red hair, green eyes, etc. These people have some parts that look alike, but they are not related. Words work the same way. Words are related if there is something about their meaning that is the same. Encourage students to think of ways the words they generate might be in the same meaning family.

1. Select a content word to study and write it on the board.

2. Ask students to pronounce the word and see if they know any other words that look and sound like it.

3. List words students think of, and underline the parts that look and sound the same.

4. Have students pronounce the words, emphasizing the parts that are pronounced the same. Point out that thinking of a word that looks and sounds the same as a new word will help them remember how to pronounce and spell the new word.

5. Circle the words that are related to the starting word (words with morphemic relationships). Point out that related words help with determining the meaning of the starting word.

 Hint: Look at your state standards and determine whether the standard refers to the term **root word** or **base word**. Use that term in your lessons so that students will recognize it on an assessment.

If the content word you select is **transformation**, students might say the following words look like and sound like **transformation**:

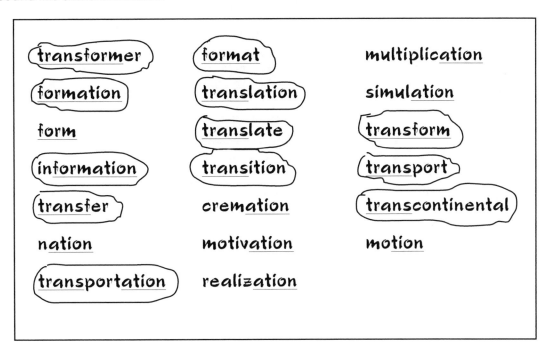

 Note: Teachers who use Word Detectives in their classrooms find that having a clear definition before they start the lesson helps them as students look for relationships among the words. The definition is not provided for students to memorize.

Note: This is just a sample word for Word Detectives. The lesson you teach should use a content word from your curriculum. This will help students learn to use familiar parts of words to decode and determine meanings when possible.

Hint: Because transfer of all word activities is crucial, we occasionally ask students to write about how they will use the information learned from Word Detectives in their daily reading and writing. Have students write this in the Working with Words section of their Big-Blocks Notebooks.

Word Detectives Homework
Option 1: Type the words students brainstormed in the Word Detectives lesson or write them on the reproducible provided on page 154. Have students take home the words and sort them, add category headings, and add any additional words they can think of. Students can create their own categories or you can provide the categories for them.

Option 2: Type the words students brainstormed in the Word Detectives lesson or write the words on the reproducible provided on page 155 and have students write any corresponding root words.

Goal Two: Word Wall Words

Selecting Word Wall Words
1. Gather several writing samples from each student during the first few days of school.

2. Look at the spelling errors students make and compare them to the list of priority spelling words on pages 126–130. First and second priority words should be introduced first to give students the most opportunities to practice and relearn them during the year.

3. Select 8–10 words that most students misspelled in their writing samples to practice this month. Use one 20-minute lesson to introduce the words to your students.

Introducing Word Wall Words
It isn't enough simply to post the most commonly misspelled words. Students must actively engage in writing and spelling the words correctly.

1. As you introduce the words to be learned, explain to students that in English, many of the most common words are not spelled logically. Have students look at each word and tell you what is illogical about it. Use questions to help them see that these words don't follow the usual patterns. Share with students what you know about the brain and automatic learning (see page 15). Convince students that the problem is not with them but with the illogical nature of some English spellings. Let students know that with your help and lots of practice, they can "rewire their brains" to spell these words correctly.

Note: A brief explanation for the illogical spelling of all First Priority: High-Frequency, Commonly Misspelled Words can be found on pages 126–128.

2. After discussing what makes the spelling of a new word illogical, ask students to say the letters in the word aloud in a rhythmic, chanting fashion. Students (and you) may be uncomfortable with this at first, but it is a vital part of relearning. The brain responds to sound and rhythm. Think of the number of jingles and raps you know. You remember these easily because they are set to short, rhythmic tunes or beats. Words may be chanted cheerleader style, clapped, snapped, tapped, etc.

3. Once all of the new words have been chanted, have students write the words with careful attention to each letter and the sequences of the letters in each word. Don't assign students to write each word five times. They will do this "mechanically" without attending to the individual letters. They may even spell them incorrectly five times, which only compounds the problem! The words should be printed in manuscript, not written in cursive. Words that are to be committed to memory for later use should always be printed for easier recall.

Hint: If your curriculum requires cursive writing instruction, you can have students write the words in cursive beside the printed words. This extra step would be for handwriting practice, not spelling practice.

4. Have students check the words by chanting their spellings again as they touch each letter.

5. Display the Word Wall words, arranged by first letter, somewhere in the room. Post new words on the Word Wall once they have been introduced. You will begin the year with a blank wall. After the first month, there will be 8–10 words; after the second month, there will be 16–20 words, etc.

Introduce the words in a 20-minute lesson. It is preferable that the writing occur in the context of the initial introduction. This means that all modes of instruction are employed to teach the new words: visual (looking at the posted words), auditory (chanting), and kinesthetic (writing).

Hint: To post the words on the wall, write the words on index cards or construction paper. Using different colors makes them more visible and attractive. This is particularly helpful for easily confused words (for example, **their/they're/there**). If you use a computer to create the word cards, try the Comic Sans font in 150 point.

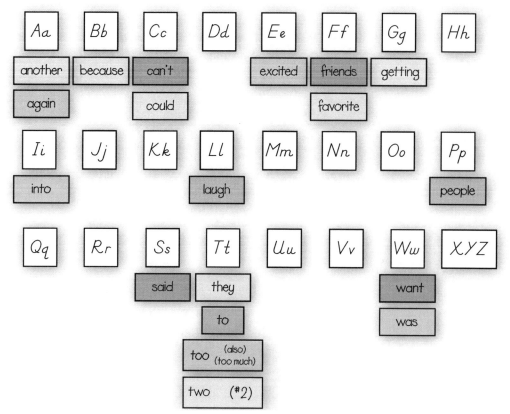

Some of the Word Wall words you introduce will have spelling changes. It will be helpful to underline or highlight the spelling changes on the posted words so that students can transfer that information to other words they read and spell. Meanings of homophones are more easily learned when meaning clues are provided. (See **too** and **two** in the example above.)

Word Wall Review Activities

Throughout the month, look for a few spare minutes to review these 8–10 words. Chant them or write them each once to keep students thinking about the new words. You may also review Word Wall words using riddles.

Word Wall Riddles

Word Wall Riddles, like Nifty Thrifty Fifty Riddles, focus students on a particular feature of each word through a riddle. Here are directions for riddles:

1. Have each student number a piece of paper from 1–8 (or the number of words you have time to review).

2. Give students clues to the words you want them to write.

3. Have students print the word that matches each riddle.

For example, if you have placed the word **you're** on your Word Wall, the riddle might be, "Write the contraction for **you are**." Complete directions for reviewing words using riddles can be found on page 23.

Goal Three: Visual Checking System

What Looks Right?

A good writer generally writes a word the way she thinks it should be spelled, then decides if it "looks right." If it does, she continues to write. If it doesn't, she checks the spelling in a dictionary. What Looks Right? lessons help students use these important self-monitoring strategies.

1. Begin by writing two words on the board that have the same sound pattern, but different spelling patterns (for example, **bite** and **fight**).

2. Point out the rhyme with different spelling patterns. Tell students that good spellers use a visual checking strategy to see if a word "looks right." If it doesn't look right, good spellers try another spelling pattern for the rhyme. If a writer needs to be sure, he looks it up in the dictionary.

3. Create two columns on a piece of chart paper or a transparency. Write the words as the column headings. Have each student do the same on a sheet of paper.

4. Tell students that you are going to say and write words using both spelling patterns. Their job is to decide which one looks right and write only that one in the correct column. Then, they will find the word in the dictionary to "prove" it is the correct spelling.

5. Once students have proven their spellings are correct, erase or cross out the incorrect spellings on the chart or overhead.

Your Chart

bite	fight
~~plite~~	plight
~~flite~~	flight
quite	~~quight~~
site	sight

Student Paper

bite	fight
	plight
	flight
quite	
site	sight

ear	cheer
carear	career
appear	appeer
reindear	reindeer
pionear	pioneer
overhear	overheer
enginear	engineer
reappear	reappeer
voluntear	volunteer
disappear	disappeer
multiyear	multiyeer
musketear	musketeer

Goal Four: Cross-Checking

Guess the Covered Word

Guess the Covered Word has students cross-check meaning (including structure), word length, and all of the beginning letters up to the first vowel to figure out words in a game-like activity. Lessons may be developed using content texts or literature selections.

1. To create a Guess the Covered Word lesson, copy a paragraph from a text or paraphrase a text students will read or have already read. The paragraph may be copied onto an overhead transparency, chart paper, or placed under a document camera. You may copy the selection by hand or use a copier. If you choose to use a copier with a transparency, you may want to enlarge the page so that it is easier to read.

2. Select a key vocabulary word that begins with a consonant in each sentence of the paragraph. Cover that word with two torn self-stick notes. The first note should cover all of the beginning consonant letters up to the first vowel (onset) and the second note should cover the remaining letters in the word (rime).

3. Read each sentence and have students make 3–4 guesses for the missing word with all of the letters covered. Write down these guesses. If a student offers a guess that does not make sense in the context of the sentence or would not fit in the covered space, don't write it down. Instead, remind them that they are answering the questions, "What makes sense?" and "What looks right?" Guide students to make appropriate guesses.

4. Remove the self-stick note that covers the beginning letter(s) (onset). Erase or cross out any guesses that don't begin with the correct consonant(s).

5. Have students make additional guesses for the word that not only make sense but also have all of the correct beginning letters.

6. After 3–4 guesses that meet both criteria, reveal the rest of the word and see if anyone guessed the covered word.

Here is a passage from *The Revolutionary War* by Brendan January (Children's Press, 2001) that could be used for a Guess the Covered Word lesson. The covered words are printed in bold.

The Stamp Act

In 1765, Parliament **passed** the Stamp Act. This law said that all **printed** paper would cost extra money. The new tax law angered the people in the **colonies**. The colonists thought it was unfair because they were not allowed to vote on any **decisions** made by Parliament. The colonists were afraid they might lose their **freedom**. Colonial leaders sent letters to King George III and **Parliament**, asking them to remove the hated tax.

October

Month at a Glance

It is now October. Beginning-of-the-year expectations have been established and students are into the necessary routines. Their first draft writing is still reviewed to select the words necessary for the Word Wall and to make sure that they are correctly spelling the words already posted on the Word Wall.

In Working with Words, students learn to look at the Word Wall to verify that they have spelled the Word Wall words correctly and to look for morphemes and root words they need from the Nifty Thrifty Fifty words. They are noticing many more words that have morphemes as they read and frequently want to share with you.

Here are the major things you will do during Working with Words in October to help students move toward meeting all four goals:

- **Goal One:** Polysyllabic Words

  Add seven more Nifty Thrifty Fifty words to the Word Wall. Use riddles to review the words. Introduce Mini-WORDO, a new review activity. Use the suggested Word Sort to extend understanding of **dis**- words. Use the suggested Root Word lesson to extend understanding of the root word **cover**. Use the first Scavenger Hunt to review -**y** words. Have students use the Nifty Thrifty Fifty Cards to explore combinations of prefixes, suffixes, and root words for all 15 words. Use the Making Words lesson to work with the suffixes -**ent** and -**ly**, the prefix **in**-, and the root word **depend**. Use the Word Detectives lesson to help students use the prefixes and suffixes of content-area words to determine meanings.

- **Goal Two:** Word Wall Words

  Choose 8–10 more words from students' writing and add these to the Word Wall. Use spare minutes to review and practice all of the words through chanting and writing, or with Word Wall Riddles. Introduce Be a Mind Reader, a new review activity. Hold students accountable for the Word Wall words in all of their writing.

- **Goal Three:** Visual Checking System

  Use the What Looks Right? lesson to focus on the **tion** and **sion** patterns.

- **Goal Four:** Cross-Checking

  Use Guess the Covered Word lessons to introduce content-area vocabulary or highlight a part of speech. This month, you might consider choosing excerpts from science texts.

Goal One: Polysyllabic Words

Words with three or more syllables follow patterns that are more sophisticated than words whose patterns are onsets and rimes. These word features require that students understand how words change in their spelling, pronunciation, and meaning as suffixes and prefixes are added.

Nifty Thrifty Fifty Words

Introducing Nifty Thrifty Fifty Words

1. Talk about meaning and determine the root, prefix, suffix, and any spelling changes.

2. Say the letters in each word aloud in a rhythmic, chanting fashion.

3. Have students write each word one time, paying attention to the letters and the sequence of letters.

4. Check words by having students say them again in a rhythmic chant, touching each letter as they say it.

5. Post the new words on the Word Wall under their beginning letters.

See page 22 for complete directions for introducing Nifty Thrifty Fifty Words.

expensive: Expensive is the word **expense** with the suffix **-ive** added and the final **e** dropped. Related words are **expend** and **expense**. **Expend/expense/expensive** are related in the same way as **defend/defense/defensive** and **offend/offense/offensive**.

governor: This is the root word **govern** with the suffix **-or**. Like **-er**, the suffix **-or** often signifies a person or thing that does something. The governor governs; the donor donates; the actor acts.

impression: Impression is the root word **press** with the prefix **im-** and the suffix **-ion**. **Press** is a common root meaning "exerting pressure." Footprints in the snow make an impression. The impression your attitude makes on people is pressed into their minds. Related words are **depress/depression** (things are pressed down) and **compress/compression** (things are pressed together). The prefix **im-** means "in, into, toward, or within." Other words where **im-** means "in, into, toward, or within" include **immigrants** and **imports**. Remind students that **im-** can also signal an opposite relationship, as in the Nifty Thrifty Fifty word **impossible** that they learned in August/September.

independence: This is the root word **depend** with the prefix **in-** and the suffix **-ence**. Help students see that independence is the opposite of dependence. The prefix **in-**, like **im-** (impossible), often signals an opposite relationship, as in **inactive** and **inconvenient**. The **depend/dependent/dependence** relationship occurs in many words, including **differ/different/difference**, **innocent/innocence**, and **patient/patience**.

submarine: Submarine is the root word **marine** with the prefix **sub-**. **Marine** means "water" and **sub-** means "under." Submarines go under the water. Other **sub-** words in which **sub-** means under or below include **subfreezing**, **submerge**, and **subway**.

transportation: Students will probably see the word **transport** with the suffix **-ation**. However, the root word is **port**, which means "bring or carry." Students can relate the meaning of **port** to **export** in which you carry out, **import** in which you carry in, and **report**, in which you bring information back. The prefix **trans-** means "across or through." When you carry things across a place, you **transport** them. Other words in which **trans-** means "across or through" include **transatlantic** and **transfusion**. Other examples of -**ation** words include **fascination** and **registration**.

unfinished: Students should notice the root word **finish** with the -**ed** ending. The prefix **un-** often changes a word to its opposite meaning, as in **unfriendly** and **unhappy**. The ending -**ed** puts a word in past tense, as in **walked**, **raised**, **baked**, and **stumbled**.

Nifty Thrifty Fifty Review Activities
Nifty Thrifty Fifty Riddles
Use riddles to review the Nifty Thrifty Fifty words, prefixes, roots, and suffixes. Have each student number a piece of paper from 1 to 7 (or the number of words you have time to review). Give the following clues for the new Nifty Thrifty Fifty words introduced this month.

1. Write the word that describes an elected official. (governor)
2. Write the word that has a prefix that means "opposite" and a suffix that means "something already happened." (unfinished)
3. Write the word with a prefix meaning under. (submarine)
4. Write the word that means "something that costs a lot of money." (expensive)
5. Write the word that has a prefix that means "across or through." (transportation)
6. Write the four-syllable word that means the opposite of dependence. (independence)
7. Write the word with the root word **press**. (impression)

Have each student check her own paper by chanting the letters aloud once more and underlining each letter as she says it.

Nifty Thrifty Fifty Mini-WORDO
Mini-WORDO is a game that is played like bingo. Use this game to review Nifty Thrifty Fifty words and word parts.

1. For this review, each student will need a blank Mini-WORDO card. (A reproducible is provided on page 133.)
2. Tell students the nine Nifty Thrifty Fifty words to review. (See page 38 for the October words.) Have students write each one of the words in the box of their choice. Check to make sure that they spell each word correctly.

expensive	governor	impression
independence	submarine	unfinished
transportation	discovery	encouragement

3. One at a time, say and show combined words that are made up of the parts studied so far. (See below for possible combined words to call out for October.)

4. Students will cover any word on their cards that contains a word part also contained in the called word. (For example, when you call out **expression**, students will cover **expensive** and **impression**.)

5. Once a student has three covered words in a row (across, down, or diagonally), he says, "Wordo." If each of the words he covered on his card match part of a word that you have called, he is the winner.

Have students write the following Nifty Thrifty Fifty words on their blank Mini-WORDO cards:

expensive	transportation	independence	discovery	encouragement
governor	impression	unfinished	submarine	

Possible combined words to call out for October:

government	express	subbed	finished	importation	transported
inexpensive	discovered	encouraged	uncovered	expression	depended

Beyond Nifty Thrifty Fifty

Nifty Thrifty Fifty Cards

Have students write the prefixes, roots, and suffixes introduced this month on individual cards. Using all of the word cards written to date, guide students in making two new words using prefixes, roots, and suffixes. After making the words you suggest, ask each student to make a new word on his own. Next, give students a neologism to make and to define. After making the neologism you suggest, ask each student to make a new neologism on her own. For more information and directions for Nifty Thrifty Fifty Cards, see page 24. Students should write the following morphemes on index cards:

prefix	root	suffix
ex-	**expense	-ive
	govern	-or
*im-	press	-sion
in-	depend	-ence
sub-	marine	
trans-	port	-ation
*un-	finish	-ed

*These morpheme cards were made for a previous word. ** With some of the unpeelable prefix words, students will need to write the prefix separately, but the root word will include the prefix. **Expense** can be used to build other words, but **pense** will have no meaning for students and will likely remain unused.

Words to make: inexpensive, transposed

Ask students to make their own words from the morphemes.

Neologism to make: transpressor

Ask a student to use the word in a sensible sentence. Be sure the sentence defines the word as "someone or something that presses things through or among several people or things." For example, "The senator was the **transpressor** of this bill."

Ask students to make their own neologisms. Suggest that they make up riddles or say sentences that will help other students discover the spelling and meaning of their neologisms.

Nifty Thrifty Fifty Cards Homework
Have each student take home the October Morpheme Chart (page 134) to help them make two additional words and one additional neologism. Have students write riddles or defining sentences for their neologisms.

Word Sorts
Word Sorts help students connect the morphemes learned in the Nifty Thrifty Fifty to words that occur in their independent reading and in their content-area studies.

Prefix and Suffix Sorts
1. Write column headings. In each heading, include the meaning of the morpheme or what the morpheme does to the root word. In columns where the chunk is not a morpheme, indicate whether it aids spelling and pronunciation, or is only part of the word.

-sion (suffix) verb becomes noun	part of the word spelling/ pronunciation

2. Have each student create a page in the Working With Words section of his Big-Blocks Notebook with the same labeled columns and examples you have, or provide the corresponding reproducible (pages 141–149) for students to add to their Big-Blocks Notebooks. Students will underline the common part in each word.

3. Write words in the first row that students will recognize and are good examples of words with the morpheme. Include examples of words that look and sound like they would have that morpheme but don't. Be sure to use the Nifty Thrifty Fifty word that connects to the morpheme as your example.

4. Discuss why these words are in each column. Use the Nifty Thrifty Fifty explanation for the example word and describe why the "part of the word spelling/pronunciation" word is not an example.

For example, if your Word Sort chart looks like this,

-sion (suffix) verb becomes noun	part of the word spelling/ pronunciation
invasion	session

then the conversation you have with students may sound like this: "Invasion is the word **invade** with the -**sion** suffix. The spelling and pronunciation change is common for many words ending in **d-e**. The verb **invade** becomes the noun **invasion** when the -**sion** suffix is added. **Session** is not an example of a word with the -**sion** suffix. When you take off the -**sion** , **ses** isn't a word and doesn't make sense."

5. Now, show and pronounce the first word students should write on the chart. Use it in a sentence and model why it belongs in the first column. For example, "This word is **permission**. I gave my daughter permission to go to the dance. Permission is made from **permit**. When I give permission, I permit her to go. Since I can think of the verb **permit** that goes with the noun **permission**, I can put permission in the first column. This word is **mansion**. She lives in a mansion on a hill. I know that mansion does not come from **man**, so I will write it in the second column."

6. Tell students that you will show and say some words. They will write each word in the column where they think it belongs. After each word, have students tell you where the word belongs and how it fits in that category.

7. End the lesson by helping students see how knowing the ways a prefix or suffix affects words will help them when they encounter new words beginning or ending with those letters.

Occasionally, end a Word Sort lesson by writing a sentence that contains an unfamiliar word with the word part that was studied. Ask students to use the context and the information learned to determine if the word part helped with meaning, spelling and pronunciation only, or if the word part was only part of the word but not pronounced the same. For example, after doing a Word Sort lesson for the suffix -**sion**, students might consider this sentence:

The **tension** in the room was caused by the awkward situation.

Then, students decide and describe how they decoded and found meaning for the word **tension**. They can either share their ideas verbally or write these explanations in their Big-Blocks Notebooks.

 Hint: On occasion, it is also important to ask students to write about how they will use the information learned from Word Sorts in their daily reading and writing. Have them write this in the Working with Words section of their Big-Blocks Notebooks.

October Word Sorts

Prefix Sort: dis-

(from the Nifty Thrifty Fifty word **discovery**, introduced in August/September)

dis- (prefix) against, opposite, or apart	spelling/pronunciation only	part of the word/ different pronunciation

See page 141 for a reproducible of this prefix sort. To introduce this sort you might say, "**Discovery** is the root word **cover** with the prefix **dis-** and the suffix -**y**. The root word **cover** can mean 'to hide something.' The prefix **dis-** often changes a word to an opposite form. It can also mean 'apart.' Therefore, when you **discover** something, it is no longer hidden. **Discovery** fits in the first column. **Distinct** begins like **discovery**; however, **tinct** isn't a root word, so **distinct** fits in the second column. **Dishes** begins with the letters **d-i-s** but doesn't sound like the prefix **dis-** in **discovery**, so **dishes** belongs in the third column."

Show and say the following words one at a time and have students put each word in the correct column:

disconnect	dishonest	dishware	discontinue	disappear
discipline	disability	dismal	disagree	discourage
district	disorganized	distance	disobey	disaster
dissatisfied	distrust	disco	dismay	

dis- (prefix) against, opposite, or apart	spelling/pronunciation only	part of the word/ different pronunciation
discovery	distinct	dishes
disconnect	dismay	dishware
dishonest	discipline	dismal
discontinue	district	disaster
disappear	distance	
disability	disco	
disagree		
discourage		
disorganized		
disobey		
dissatisfied		
distrust		

Root Word Lessons

Word lessons that focus on root words allow students to see how knowing the root of a word sometimes helps them decode the meaning of a new word. Choose a root word that has many recognizable words associated with it. Students often enjoy seeing how many words they can read and write from just one root.

1. Write the root word on the board.
2. Talk about what the word means.
3. Write several more words that have the root word in them.
4. Have students pronounce the words. Talk about how the meaning of the root word changes.
5. After you provide multiple examples, ask students if they can think of more.

Root Word Lesson: cover

(from the Nifty Thrifty Fifty word **discovery**, introduced in August/September)

Definition: to put something over

Write these words:

cover   bedcover   coverless

Students might suggest:

recover	uncover	covers	discover	discovery	cover-up
coverage	coveralls	dustcover	hardcover	recoveries	slipcover

Scavenger Hunt

Sometime during the month, have students use their reading texts for a Scavenger Hunt. Have them find words that have an identified prefix, suffix, or spelling change represented by one of the Nifty Thrifty Fifty words introduced to date. Have students record their findings on a piece of chart paper posted in the classroom.

1. Identify a prefix, suffix, or spelling change for students to find in their reading this week.

2. Make a chart to record the words students find. Begin by writing a representative word from a Guided Reading selection or one of the common words suggested in the monthly activities.

3. During the week, have students write words they find onto the chart and write their initials after them.

4. On the day of the Scavenger Hunt lesson, direct students to look closely at the words on the chart.

   • Use two different colors of markers to identify the root and affix of each word on the chart.

- If there is a spelling change, write what changed above the root. (See below for an example.)

- Cross off any word students agree does not have a prefix, suffix, or spelling change.

- Assign students to look up words that they are not sure about or that the class does not agree on. (This should happen at least once in the context of the 20-minute lesson.)

The suggested Scavenger Hunt lesson for October deals with words ending in the **-y** suffix. If a student reads *The Lucky Stone* by Lucille Clifton (Yearling, 1986), she might add the following **-y** words to the Scavenger Hunt chart:

story	mighty
lady	Great-granddaddy
pretty	ruffly
lucky	eighty

At the end of the Scavenger Hunt lesson, the root words will be highlighted (or written) in one color and the **-y** suffix will be highlighted (or written) in another color. The spelling change for **ruffly** should be written over its root. The words **story**, **lady**, **pretty**, and **Great-grandaddy** should be crossed off since they are not examples of the **-y** suffix.

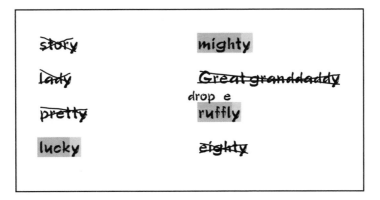

 Hint: Occasionally ask students to write about how they will use the information learned from the Scavenger Hunt in their daily reading and writing. Have students write this in the Working with Words section of their Big-Blocks Notebooks.

Scavenger Hunt Homework

Have each student find three or more words that end with **-y** (or the morpheme you have chosen) in his reading. Have students place checkmarks by words they know are examples of the **-y** suffix, cross off words they are sure are not **-y** examples, and leave blank any words they aren't sure about. Then, have students look up in the dictionary any words that haven't been marked. Have students turn in their homework papers with all of the words either marked with a checkmark or crossed off.

Hint: Select a reasonable number of words for students to find. Take into consideration the complexity of the morpheme and the likelihood that it will show up in students' independent reading materials.

Here is a Scavenger Hunt example using *Heaven* by Angela Johnson (Simon Pulse, 2000).

Making Words

In this activity, students will learn how adding letters and moving letters around creates new words. Prior to the lesson, write or type the words students will make. To begin the lesson, give each student a copy of the corresponding letter strip (page 150) and have him cut or tear the letters apart. Have students write the matching uppercase letter on the back of each letter. See page 25 for complete directions for Making Words.

independently

Letters: e e e i d d l n n p t y

Make Words: Ned, need, deed, deep, nine, line, needy, deeply, indent, depend, ninety, nineteen, dependent, independent, independently

Directions:

- Tell students how many letters to use to make each word.

- Emphasize how changing just one letter or rearranging letters makes a different word.

   "Add a letter to **Ned** to spell **need**."

   "Change one letter in **nine** to spell **line**."

- When students are not just adding or changing one letter, cue them to start over.

  "Start over and use six letters to spell **indent**."

- Give meaning or sentence clues when needed to clarify the word they are making.

  "Start over and use five letters to spell **needy**. 'Our class brought in canned food and made a Thanksgiving basket for a **needy** family.'"

- Give students one minute to figure out the secret word, then give clues if needed.

  "Our secret word is related to the word **depend**."

Sort: Sort related words and use sentence clues to show how they are related.

need, needy

"When someone is often in **need**, we say he is **needy**."

deep, deeply

"To dig a **deep** hole, you dig **deeply** into the soil."

nine, ninety, nineteen

"These numbers are related to **nine**: **ninety** and **nineteen**."

depend, dependent, independent, independently

"When you **depend** on someone, you are **dependent**."

"When you do something in an **independent** way, you did it **independently**."

Sort rhymes:

need	**nine**
deed	**line**

Reading Transfer: proceed, confine

Tell students, "Pretend you are reading and come to a new word." Have them put the words under the appropriate rhymes and use the rhymes to decode them.

Spelling Transfer: sunshine, nosebleed

Tell students, "Pretend you are writing and need to spell each of these words." Have students tell you how each word begins. Then, have students find and use the appropriate rhymes to finish spelling each new word.

Making Words Homework

See page 28 for complete Making Words Homework directions. See page 153 for a Making Words Homework reproducible. Send home the letters for **independently** with students to make and remake words.

Word Detectives

Word Detectives is an activity that encourages students to answer the questions:

Do I know any other words that look and sound like this word?

Are any of these look-alike/sound-alike words related to each other?

See page 28 for complete Word Detectives directions.

If the content word you select is **reconstruction**, students might say that the following words look like and sound like **reconstruction**:

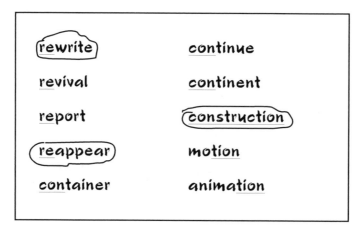

Underline the parts that look similar and circle the related words. Remind students that related words often help in determining the meaning of the chosen content word.

Word Detectives Homework

See page 30 for complete Word Detectives Homework directions. Type the words students generate in the Word Detectives lesson or use the reproducibles on pages 154 or 155 to record them.

Option 1: Have students sort the words, add category headings, and add any additional words they know.

Option 2: Have students write the root word for each word on the list that has a root word.

Goal Two: Word Wall Words

Look at student writing samples collected over the past couple of weeks. Compare student errors to the words on the Priority Word Lists found on pages 126–130. Select 8–10 words from these lists to introduce and add to the Word Wall. Introduce the words by having students:

1. Look at each word and tell you what is illogical or tricky about its spelling.

2. Say the letters in each word aloud in a rhythmic, chanting fashion.

3. Print each word once with careful attention to each letter and the sequence of the letters.

4. Check the words by chanting their spellings again as they touch each letter.

Post the new words on the Word Wall. See page 30 for complete Word Wall directions.

Word Wall Review Activities

Throughout the month, look for a few spare minutes to review these 8–10 words. Have students chant or write each word once to keep them thinking about the new words.

Here are some other Word Wall review ideas:

Word Wall Riddles

See page 23 for complete directions for reviewing words using riddles.

Riddles focus students on a particular feature of each word in a game-like activity. For example, if you have placed the word **their** on your Word Wall, a good riddle for the word might be, "Write the word that would fit in this sentence: 'That is _____ dog.'"

 Note: You should select Word Wall words based on students' spelling needs. Word Wall Riddles should be used to review the words students need to practice most.

Word Wall Be a Mind Reader

Be a Mind Reader is a favorite review activity with students. For this activity, select a word on the wall and give students five clues about the word so that they can guess it.

1. Have students number their papers from 1–5. Tell them that you are going to see who can read your mind and figure out which of the Word Wall words you are thinking of. By the fifth clue, everyone should know the word.

2. The first clue is always the same: "It is a word on the Word Wall."

3. Students should write any word they think might be your word next to number one.

4. Each succeeding clue will narrow the possibilities until the fifth and final clue, when there is only one possible word. Clues may include any features of the words you want students to notice. For example, "It has nine letters," "It has a prefix," "It has three syllables," or "It doesn't have a suffix." Since each clue builds on the previous clues, students must be good listeners and spellers.

5. As you give the clues, students should continue to write their guesses next to each number. If a succeeding clue confirms the word the student has written next to a number, then that student may write the same word next to the following number.

6. The last clue may have the word omitted from a sentence. "It fits in the sentence, 'They brought _____ brother to school.'"

If the word **they** is on your Word Wall, your Be a Mind Reader lesson clues might sound like this:

1. It is a word on the Word Wall.
2. It has one syllable.
3. It rhymes with words it doesn't look like.
4. It begins with a **t**.
5. It fits in the sentence, "I think ____ are over there."

Goal Three: Visual Checking System

What Looks Right?

What Looks Right? lessons help students use two important self-monitoring strategies: writing a word the way the writer thinks it should be spelled and checking it in a dictionary. See page 33 for complete What Looks Right? directions.

motion	pension
pention	pension
digestion	digession
migration	migrasion
dimention	dimension
nomination	nominasion
plantation	plantasion
legislation	legislasion
calculation	calculasion
preservation	preservasion
civilization	civilazasion
comprehention	comprehension

Goal Four: Cross-Checking

Guess the Covered Word

Guess the Covered Word is a guided activity in which students cross-check meaning (including structure), word length, and all of the beginning letters up to the first vowel to figure out words in a game-like activity. See page 34 for complete Guess the Covered Word directions.

Here is a possible Guess the Covered Word lesson from *Weather* by Seymour Simon (HarperTrophy, 2000):

Weather

The weather of a region changes **sharply** every time a front and the air mass behind it pass over. Cold fronts move more **rapidly** than do warm fronts. When a cold front nears, the cold air forms a sort of a **wedge** and pushes the warm air aloft. **Towering** clouds form quickly and it may begin to rain or snow heavily. In a few hours, after the rain stops, the sky usually clears and the temperature **drops**.

November

Month at a Glance

By November, you will notice that students are looking to the Word Wall for assistance when needed. Your students are anxious to share words they find in their reading that have the same morphemes as those you have studied. By chanting and writing these words, students begin to spell more of the words correctly. You are still holding them accountable by marking **WW** on any misspelled words and making sure that students correct them. This month, a new review activity, Nifty Thrifty Fifty Be a Mind Reader, is added.

Here are the major things you will do during Working with Words in November to help students move toward meeting all four goals:

- **Goal One:** Polysyllabic Words

  Add seven more Nifty Thrifty Fifty words to the Word Wall. Use Be a Mind Reader, Riddles, and Mini-WORDO to review the words. Use the suggested Word Sort to extend the understanding of the suffix -**ly** and the prefix **im**-. Use the Scavenger Hunt to review -**ment** words. Have students use the Nifty Thrifty Fifty Cards to explore combinations of prefixes, suffixes, and root words for all 22 words. Use the Making Words lesson to work with the suffix -**ian** and the root word **electric**. Use the Word Detectives lesson to help students use the prefixes and suffixes of content-area words to determine meanings.

- **Goal Two:** Word Wall Words

  Choose 8–10 more words from students' writing and add these to the Word Wall. Use spare minutes to review and practice all of the words through chanting and writing, Word Wall Riddles, and Be a Mind Reader activities. Hold students accountable for these words in all of their writing.

- **Goal Three:** Visual Checking System

  Use the What Looks Right? lesson to focus on the **ade**, **aid**, and **ayed** patterns.

- **Goal Four:** Cross-Checking

  Use the Guess the Covered Word lessons to introduce content-area vocabulary or highlight a part of speech. This month, you might consider adapting a paragraph from a favorite author.

Goal One: Polysyllabic Words

Studying words with sophisticated patterns helps students understand how words change in their spelling, pronunciation, and meaning as suffixes and prefixes are added.

Nifty Thrifty Fifty Words

Introduce the following new words. See page 22 for complete directions for introducing Nifty Thrifty Fifty words.

beautiful: Beautiful is the root **beauty** with the suffix -**ful** and the **y** changed to an **i**. The suffix -**ful** means "full of," as in **painful** and **fearful**. If the word to which -**ful** is being added ends in **y**, the **y** will change to **i**, as in **merciful** and **plentiful**. Other examples of -**ful** words are **forgetful**, **hateful**, and **capful**.

classify: Classify is the root word **class** with the suffix -**ify**. Other words with -**ify** include **glory/glorify**, **sign/signify**, **note/notify**, and **false/falsify**.

community: Community is the root word **unity** with the prefix **com-** and the **m** doubled. **Com-** means "with or together." People who live in a community live together in unity. Other words in which the **com-** indicates "with or together" include **compose** (to put together), **combat** (to do battle with), and **compress** (to press together).

communities: The plural of **community** has the **y** changed to **i** before adding the suffix -**es**. Other examples include **country/countries**, **county/counties**, and **city/cities**.

electricity: This is the root word **electric** with the -**ity** suffix. Note that the spelling does not change, but the pronunciation of the **c** does. (Remember, it is the pronunciation of the **c** that changes in **music/musician**. **C** is a tricky letter. You have to expect it to assume many different identities!) Other words follow the **electric/electricity** pattern, including **public/publicity** and **toxic/toxicity**.

happiness: Happiness is the root word **happy** with the suffix -**ness** and the **y** changed to **i**. Other words with -**ness** include **darkness**, **goodness**, and **friendliness**.

prettier: This is **pretty** with the suffix -**er** added. The suffix -**er** can mean "more or greater." The **y** in **pretty** is changed to **i** before the suffix is added. Other words where -**er** means "more than" include **uglier**, **smarter**, and **greater**.

Nifty Thrifty Fifty Review Activities

Nifty Thrifty Fifty Be a Mind Reader

Nifty Thrifty Fifty Be a Mind Reader, like Word Wall Be a Mind Reader, is an activity in which you select a word from the wall, then give students five clues about that word so that they can guess it.

1. Have students number their papers from 1–5.

2. Give them the first clue, which is always, "It's a Nifty Thrifty Fifty word."

3. Students should write any word they think might be your word next to number one.

4. Each succeeding clue will narrow the possibilities until the fifth and final clue, when there is only one possible word. Clues may include any features of the word you want students to notice. For example, "It has nine letters," "It has a prefix," "It has three syllables," or "It doesn't have a suffix."

5. As you give the clues, students should continue to write their guesses next to each number.

Here are some examples for November:

1. It is a Nifty Thrifty Fifty word.
2. It has three syllables.
3. It has a prefix and a suffix.
4. The prefix means "opposite." (unfriendly, unfinished)
5. It means the same as **incomplete**. (unfinished)

1. It is a Nifty Thrifty Fifty word.
2. It only has a suffix.
3. It has a double consonant.
4. It has three syllables. (happiness, classify, prettier)
5. It means "to put into categories." (classify)

1. It is a Nifty Thrifty Fifty word.
2. It has no spelling change.
3. It has less than 10 letters.
4. It only has a suffix. (governor, hopeless, musician, richest)
5. Its suffix means "without." (hopeless)

1. It is a Nifty Thrifty Fifty word.
2. It has three syllables.
3. It is a noun.
4. Its suffix makes the word become a person. (musician, composer, governor)
5. It is the person in charge of a state's government. (governor)

1. It is a Nifty Thrifty Fifty word.
2. It has 10 letters.
3. It has four syllables.
4. Its prefix means "opposite." (unfriendly, unfinished, impossible)
5. It is the opposite of **possible**. (impossible)

1. It is a Nifty Thrifty Fifty word.
2. It has a prefix and a suffix.
3. It has four syllables.
4. It has five vowels. (communities, independence, transportation)
5. Its root word means "to carry" and the prefix means "across or through." (transportation)

1. It is a Nifty Thrifty Fifty word.
2. It has three syllables.
3. It is an adjective or describing word.
4. It has a suffix. (beautiful, prettier, unfriendly, expensive)
5. Its suffix compares, or means "more than." (prettier)

Nifty Thrifty Fifty Riddles

Have each student number a piece of paper to correspond with the number of words you have time to review. Give the following clues for the new Nifty Thrifty Fifty words introduced this month. See page 23 for complete directions for reviewing words using riddles.

1. Write the word with a suffix that can mean "more" and lets you compare. (prettier)
2. Write the word that has a suffix, no spelling change, and no pronunciation change. (classify)
3. Write the word with a suffix that means "more than one." (communities)
4. Write the word that means "full of beauty." (beautiful)
5. Write the word with a suffix that changes the pronunciation of the root word. (electricity)
6. Write the word that only has a prefix. (community)
7. Write the word with the root word **happy**. (happiness)

Have each student check her own paper by chanting the letters aloud once more and underlining each letter as she says it.

Nifty Thrifty Fifty Mini-WORDO

See page 37 for complete Mini-WORDO directions.

Have students write the following Nifty Thrifty Fifty words on their blank Mini-WORDO cards (page 133):

hopeless	classify	beautiful
impossible	happiness	prettier
richest	electricity	musician

Possible combined words to show and say:

hopeful	possibility	classy	happiest
electrician	beautify	prettiness	

Beyond Nifty Thrifty Fifty
Nifty Thrifty Fifty Cards

See page 24 for directions for using Nifty Thrifty Fifty Cards to make new words. Students should put the following morphemes on individual cards:

prefix	root	suffix	spelling change
	beauty	-ful	i
	class	-ify	
*com-	unity		m
*com-	unity	-es	*i
	electric	-ity	
	happy	-ness	*i
	pretty	*-er	*i

*These morpheme cards were made for a previous word.

Words to make: classiness, classification

Ask students to make their own words from the morphemes.

Neologism to make: expossibility

Ask a student to use the neologism in a sensible sentence. Be sure the sentence defines the word as "something that was possible but isn't any longer." For example, "The sold-out movie is an expossibility."

Ask students to make their own neologisms. Suggest that they make up riddles or say sentences that will help other students discover the spelling and meaning of their neologisms.

Nifty Thrifty Fifty Cards Homework

See page 25 for Nifty Thrifty Fifty Cards Homework directions. Have each student take home the November Morpheme Chart (page 135) to help them make two additional words and one additional neologism. Have students write riddles or defining sentences for their neologisms.

Word Sorts

See page 39 for complete directions for Prefix and Suffix Sorts.

Suffix Sort: -ly

(from the Nifty Thrifty Fifty word **unfriendly**, introduced in August/September)

-ly (suffix) noun to adjective	spelling/pronunciation only	part of the word/ different pronunciation

See page 142 for a reproducible of this suffix sort. To introduce this sort you might say, "The suffix -**ly** means 'resembling' and changes **friend** to **friendly** (noun to adjective). The -**ly** suffix in **unfriendly** changes the word **friend** from a noun to an adjective, so this word fits in the first column. **Folly** has an **l-y** ending but **fol** isn't a word, so **folly** fits in the second column. **Apply** ends in **l-y**. But, **app** isn't a word and the **l-y** doesn't have the same pronunciation as the **l-y** in **unfriendly,** so **apply** goes in the last column."

Show and say the following words one at a time and have students put each word in the correct column:

brotherly   briefly   monthly   jolly   barely   finely

truly   reply   happily   safely   coolly   golly

swiftly   properly   really

-ly (suffix) noun to adjective	spelling/pronunciation only	part of the word/ different pronunciation
unfriendly	folly	apply
brotherly	jolly	reply
briefly	golly	
monthly		
barely		
finely		
truly		
happily		
safely		
coolly		
swiftly		
properly		
really		

Prefix Sort: im-

(from the Nifty Thrifty Fifty word **impossible**, introduced in August/September)

im- (prefix) in	im- (prefix) opposite	spelling/pronunciation only

See page 143 for a reproducible of this prefix sort. To introduce this sort you might say, "**Impression** is the root word **press** with the prefix **im-** and the suffix **-ion** added. The prefix **im-** means 'in, into, toward, or within.' **Impossible** is the root word **possible** with the prefix **im-**. In this word, the prefix **im-** changes the word to an opposite. **Impression** means 'pressing in,' so **impression** fits in the first column. **Impossible** is the opposite of **possible**, so this word fits in the second column. **Image** begins with **i-m**, but **image** is not the opposite of the word **age**, so **image** fits in the last column."

Show and say the following words one at a time and have students put each word in the correct column:

immature   immigrant   imitator   immovable   imperfect   import

implying   impolite   important   impatient   importer   impassable

improper   impressive   improve   imperfection   impress   impure

immigration   impatience   improvement   impurity   immediate   immeasurable

imprison   impatiently

im- (prefix) in	im- (prefix) opposite	spelling/pronunciation only
impression	impossible	image
immigrant	immature	imitator
import	immovable	implying
importer	imperfect	important
impressive	impolite	improve
impress	imperfection	improvement
immigration	impatient	immediate
imprison	impassable	
	improper	
	impure	
	impatience	
	impurity	
	immeasurable	
	impatiently	

Scavenger Hunt

See page 42 for complete directions for Scavenger Hunt.

The suggested hunt for November is for words ending in the -**ment** suffix. If a student reads *Monkeying Around* by Jane Hammerslough (Scholastic Paperbacks, 2003), he might add the following -**ment** words to the Scavenger Hunt chart:

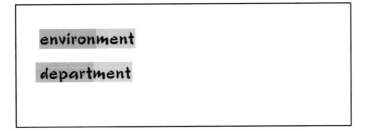

Use two different colors of markers or highlighters to identify the root and suffix of each word on the chart. If there is a spelling change, write what changed above the root. Cross off any word students agree does not have the suffix -**ment**.

Scavenger Hunt Homework

See page 44 for complete Scavenger Hunt Homework directions. Have each student find one or more words that fit this month's hunt. Here is an example using *The Sweetest Fig* by Chris Van Allsburg (Houghton Mifflin, 1993):

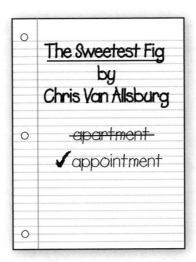

Making Words

See page 25 for complete Making Words directions.

electrician

Letters: a e e i i c c l n r t

Make Words: eat, neat, Neal/lean, rain, train, eater, eaten, clean, center, central, cleaner, trainee, electric, electrician

Directions:

- Tell students how many letters to use to make each word.

- Emphasize how changing just one letter or rearranging letters makes a different word.

  "Add a letter to **rain** to spell **train**."

  "Change one letter in **eater** to spell **eaten**."

  "Use the same letters in **Neal** to spell **lean**."

- When students are not just adding or changing one letter, cue them to start over.

  "Start over and use eight new letters to spell **electric**."

- Give meaning or sentence clues when needed to clarify the word they are making.

  "Use seven letters to spell **trainee**. 'A person who is in training is called a **trainee**.'"

- Give students one minute to figure out the secret word, then give clues if needed.

  "Our secret word is related to the word **electric**."

Sort: Sort related words and use sentence clues to show how they are related.

eat, eater, eaten

"What a good **eater** you are tonight! It is nice to see you **eat** so well. You have **eaten** all of your dinner!"

clean, cleaner

"A **cleaner** is a person who cleans or something you use to **clean**. **Cleaner** can also mean 'more **clean**.'"

train, trainee

"A person that you **train** is called a **trainee**."

electric, electrician

"An **electrician** installs and fixes **electric** wiring."

center, central

"Something located at the **center** of a place is in a **central** location."

Sort rhymes:

eat	lean	rain
neat	clean	train

Reading Transfer: defeat, complain

Tell students, "Pretend you are reading and come to a new word." Have students put the words under the appropriate rhymes and use the rhymes to decode them.

Spelling Transfer: retreat, restrain

Tell students, "Pretend you are writing and need to spell each of these words." Have students tell you how each word begins. Then, have students find and use the appropriate rhymes to finish spelling each new word.

Making Words Homework

See page 28 for complete Making Words Homework directions. See page 153 for a Making Words Homework reproducible. Send the letters for **electrician** home with students to make and remake words.

Word Detectives

See page 28 for complete Word Detectives directions. If the selected content word is **equation**, students might say the following words look like and sound like **equation**:

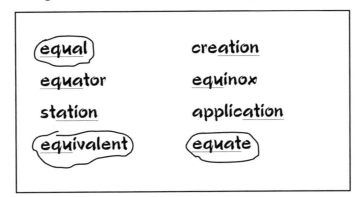

equal   creation

equator   equinox

station   application

equivalent   equate

Underline the parts that look similar and circle the related words. Remind students that related words often help in determining the meaning of the chosen content word.

Word Detectives Homework

See page 30 for complete Word Detectives Homework directions. Type the words students generate in the Word Detectives lesson or use the reproducibles on pages 154 or 155 to record them.

Option 1: Have students sort the words, add category headings, and add any additional words they know.

Option 2: Have students write the root word for each word on the list that has a root word.

Goal Two: Word Wall Words

Continue to gather students' writing samples to determine which words will be introduced and placed on the Word Wall.

- Be sure to highlight what makes the words illogical or difficult to spell.

- Students need to chant and write each word as it is introduced, then check each word by chanting their spellings as they touch each letter.

- Post the new words on the Word Wall. Hold students accountable for spelling the posted words correctly in all of their writing.

Word Wall Review Activities

Review the Word Wall words throughout the week and month with the following activities.

Word Wall Riddles

Riddles focus students' attention on particular features of each word in a game-like activity. For example, if you have placed the word **want** on your Word Wall, your riddle might be, "Write the word that completes the sentence, "I _____ to go to see a movie." See page 23 for complete directions for reviewing words using riddles.

Word Wall Be a Mind Reader

See page 47 for complete Word Wall Be a Mind Reader directions.

Select a word from the wall. Give students five clues so that they can guess the word. For example, if you have added the word **too** to your Word Wall, you might use the following Be a Mind Reader lesson:

1. It is a word on the Word Wall.
2. It has one syllable.
3. It begins with a **t**.
4. It has two vowels.
5. It fits in the sentence, "He ate _____ much ice cream."

Goal Three: Visual Checking System

What Looks Right?

See page 33 for complete What Looks Right? directions.

made	paid	played
blockade	blockaid	blockayed
bridesmade	bridesmaid	bridesmayed
charade	charaid	charayed
betrade	betraid	betrayed
lemonade	lemonaid	lemonayed
unafrade	unafraid	unafrayed
portrade	portraid	portrayed
prepade	prepaid	prepayed
replade	replaid	replayed
everglade	everglaid	everglayed

Goal Four: Cross-Checking

Guess the Covered Word

See page 34 for complete Guess the Covered Word directions. Here is a possible Guess the Covered Word lesson from *Mr. Lincoln's Way* by Patricia Polacco (Scholastic, 2003):

Parts of Speech: Verbs

As the days **passed**, Eugene never seemed to be without the book. His English teacher let Eugene **read** passages from the book in class. "I'm so pleased to **see** him reading . . . ." Mrs. Dunkle exclaimed. And when he didn't **have** his nose in that book, he was almost constantly out in the atrium! He and Mr. Lincoln **wrote** a list of plants and shrubs to buy, and types of grain and seeds to feed the birds.

December

Month at a Glance

December is a difficult month to keep things going. This is a crazy time of the year! You and your students will have to work hard to remember the importance of spelling the Word Wall words correctly and the importance of using the morphemes of the Nifty Thrifty Fifty words to figure out new words.

Here are the major things you will do during Working with Words in December to help students move toward meeting all four goals:

- **Goal One:** Polysyllabic Words

  Add seven more Nifty Thrifty Fifty words to the Word Wall. Use Be a Mind Reader, Riddles, and Mini-WORDO to review the words. Use the suggested Word Sort to extend the understanding of the prefix **en-**. Use the Scavenger Hunt to review words with the suffix **-less**. Have students use the Nifty Thrifty Fifty Cards to explore combinations of prefixes, suffixes, and root words for all 29 words. Use the Making Words lesson to work with the suffix **-tion**, the prefix **com-**, and the root word **communicate**. Use the Word Detectives lesson to help students use the prefixes and suffixes of content-area words to determine meanings.

- **Goal Two:** Word Wall Words

  Choose 8–10 more words from students' writing and add these to the Word Wall. Use spare minutes to review and practice all of the words through chanting and writing, Word Wall Riddles, and Be a Mind Reader activities. Hold students accountable for these words in all of their writing.

- **Goal Three:** Visual Checking System

  Use the What Looks Right? lesson to focus on the **ees**, **eas**, **eeze**, and **ease** patterns.

- **Goal Four:** Cross-Checking

  Use Guess the Covered Word lessons to introduce content-area vocabulary or highlight a part of speech. This month, you might consider choosing excerpts from social studies texts.

Goal One: Polysyllabic Words
Nifty Thrifty Fifty Words

Introduce the following new words. See page 22 for complete directions for introducing Nifty Thrifty Fifty words.

continuous: This is the root word **continue** with the suffix **-ous** added and the **e** dropped. The suffix **-ous** means "full of." Other common words containing a root word and **-ous** include **nervous**, **dangerous**, and **humorous**.

conversation: Conversation is the word **converse** with the suffix -**ation** added and the **e** dropped. Similar words include **reservation**, **invitation**, and **information**.

forgotten: Forgotten is the root word **forgot** with the suffix -**en** and the **t** doubled. The suffix -**en** means "cause to be or have." Similar words include **rotten**, **hidden**, and **forbidden**.

nonliving: Nonliving is the word **live** with the prefix **non-**, the suffix -**ing**, and the **e** dropped. The prefix **non-** means "the opposite," as in the words **nonfattening**, **nonsense**, and **nonfiction**.

swimming: Swimming is the root word **swim** with the suffix -**ing** and the **m** doubled. Similar words include **running**, **jogging**, **rapping**, and **drumming**.

unpleasant: Unpleasant is the word **please** with the prefix **un-**, the suffix -**ant**, and the **e** dropped. Help students notice the pronunciation change from **please** to **pleasant**. **Un-** is the most common prefix signaling an opposite. Other examples include **unable**, **unfriendly**, **unfinished**, and **undo**. Other examples of -**ant** words include **resistant**, **hesitant**, and **tolerant**.

valuable: Valuable is the word **value** with the suffix -**able** and the **e** dropped. The suffix -**able** means "worth or ability." Other words with -**able** and spelling changes are **quotable**, **likable**, and **unimaginable**.

Nifty Thrifty Fifty Review Activities
Nifty Thrifty Fifty Be a Mind Reader
See page 47 for complete Nifty Thrifty Fifty Be a Mind Reader directions.

1. It is a Nifty Thrifty Fifty word.
2. It has at least four vowels.
3. It is a noun.
4. It has three syllables. (musician, submarine)
5. It only has a prefix. (submarine)

1. It is a Nifty Thrifty Fifty word.
2. It has a prefix and a suffix.
3. It has 10 or more letters.
4. It starts with a vowel. (encouragement, independence, impression, unfinished, unfriendly, unpleasant)
5. It fits in the sentence, "The praise gave her _____ and made her want to try again." (encouragement)

1. It is a Nifty Thrifty Fifty word.
2. It has a spelling change when the suffix is added.
3. It only has a suffix.
4. It has three syllables. (forgotten, valuable)
5. The final consonant has to be doubled before adding the suffix. (forgotten)

1. It is a Nifty Thrifty Fifty word.
2. It has three syllables.
3. It has a spelling change when the suffix is added.
4. It only has a suffix. (forgotten, valuable)
5. The **e** is dropped from the root word when the suffix is added. (valuable)

1. It is a Nifty Thrifty Fifty word.
2. It has 10 or more letters.
3. It has a prefix and a suffix.
4. It begins with a **u**. (unpleasant, unfinished, unfriendly)
5. It means the opposite of friendly. (unfriendly)

1. It is a Nifty Thrifty Fifty word.
2. It has three syllables.
3. It is a person.
4. It has three vowels. (composer, governor)
5. It is someone who writes music. (composer)

1. It is a Nifty Thrifty Fifty word.
2. It is a noun.
3. It has 10 or more letters.
4. It begins with an **e**. (encouragement, electricity)
5. It only has a suffix. (electricity)

Nifty Thrifty Fifty Riddles

Have each student number a piece of paper to correspond with the number of words you have time to review. Give the following clues for the new Nifty Thrifty Fifty words introduced this month.

1. Write the word that means "when people are talking to each other." (conversation)
2. Write the word that means "something has great worth." (valuable)
3. Write the word that means "not pleasing." (unpleasant)
4. Write the word that means "not remembered." (forgotten)
5. Write the word with an opposite prefix and a spelling change before the suffix. (nonliving)
6. Write the word that has an -**ing** suffix. (swimming)
7. Write the word that means "doesn't stop." (continuous)

Have each student check his own paper by chanting the letters in each word aloud once more and underlining each letter as he says it.

Nifty Thrifty Fifty Mini-WORDO

See page 37 for Mini-WORDO directions.

Have students write the following Nifty Thrifty Fifty words on their blank Mini-WORDO cards:

forgotten	valuable	nonliving
unfriendly	unpleasant	conversation
happiness	continuous	impossible

Possible combined words to show and say:

unforgotten	unlivable	conversing	possibly
unhappy	valuation	continuation	pleasantness

Beyond Nifty Thrifty Fifty

Nifty Thrifty Fifty Cards

See page 24 for directions for using Nifty Thrifty Fifty Cards to make new words. Students should put the following morphemes on individual cards:

prefix	root	suffix	spelling change
con-	continue	-ous	
non-	live	-ing	
*con-	converse	-ation	
	swim	*-ing	*m
	value	-able	
	forgot	-en	t
*un-	please	-ant	

*These morpheme cards were made for a previous word.

Words to make: conversing, unclassifiable

Ask students to make their own words from the morphemes.

Neologism to make: nonclassable

Ask a student to use the neologism in a sensible sentence. Be sure the sentence defines the word as "something that can't be classified." For example, "The newly discovered plant is nonclassable."

Ask students to make their own neologisms. Suggest that they make up riddles or say sentences that will help other students discover the spelling and meaning of their neologisms.

December

Nifty Thrifty Fifty Cards Homework

See page 25 for complete Nifty Thrifty Fifty Cards Homework directions. Have each student take home the December Morpheme Chart (page 136) to make two additional words and one additional neologism. Have students write riddles or defining sentences for their neologisms.

Word Sorts

See page 39 for Prefix and Suffix Sorts directions.

Prefix Sort: en-

(from the Nifty Thrifty Fifty word **encouragement**, introduced in August/September)

en- (prefix) in	spelling/pronunciation only	part of the word/ different pronunciation

See page 144 for a reproducible of this suffix sort. To introduce this sort you might say, "The root word for **encouragement** is **courage**. So, **encouragement** is made of the prefix **en-**, which means 'in,' the root word **courage**, and the suffix -**ment**. **Encouragement** fits in the first column. **Enter** begins with **e-n**, but **ter** isn't a word, so **enter** fits in the second column. **Enough** begins with **e-n**. However, **ough** isn't a word and the **e-n** doesn't have the same pronunciation as the **e-n** in **encouragement**, so **enough** goes in the last column."

Show and say the following words one at a time and have students put each word in the correct column:

enthusiasm   enclose   endanger   English   entire   enlarge

enjoy   enormous   engine   energy   enrich

en- (prefix) in	spelling/pronunciation only	part of the word/ different pronunciation
encouragement	enter	enough
enclose	enthusiasm	English
endanger	entire	enormous
enlarge	engine	
enjoy	energy	
enrich		

Scavenger Hunt

See page 42 for complete Scavenger Hunt directions.

The suggested hunt for December is for words ending in the suffix -**less**. If a student reads *Boy: Tales of Childhood* by Roald Dahl (Puffin, 1999), she might add the following -**less** words to the Scavenger Hunt chart:

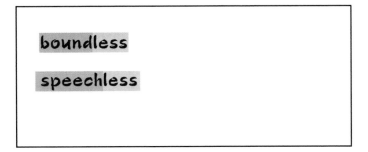

Use two different colors of markers or highlighters to identify the root and suffix of each word on the chart. If there is a spelling change, write what changed above the root. Cross off any word students agree does not have the suffix -**less**.

Scavenger Hunt Homework

See page 44 for complete Scavenger Hunt Homework directions. Have each student find two or more words that fit this month's hunt. Here is an example using *The Whipping Boy* by Sid Fleischman (Greenwillow, 1986):

December

Making Words

See page 25 for complete Making Words directions.

communications

Letters: a i i o o u c c m m n n s t

Make Words: act, out, scout, music, cousin, nation, notion, motion, action, auction/caution, suction, musician, ammunition, communications

Directions:

- Tell students how many letters to use to make each word.

- Emphasize how changing just one letter or rearranging letters makes a different word.

  "Add a letter to **action** to spell **auction**."

  "Change one letter in **notion** to spell **motion**."

  "Use the same letters in **auction** to spell **caution**."

- When students are not just adding or changing one letter, cue them to start over.

  "Start over and use six letters to spell **cousin**."

- Give meaning or sentence clues when needed to clarify the word they are making.

  "Change one letter in **nation** to spell **notion**. 'I have no **notion** where the cat might be hiding.'"

- Give students one minute to figure out the secret word, then give clues if needed.

  "Our secret word is related to the word **communicate**."

Sort: Sort related words and use sentence clues to show how they are related.

music, musician

"A **musician** plays **music**."

act, action

"To **act** is to do something. What you do is the **action**."

nation, motion, action, auction, caution, suction, ammunition, communications

You may also want to sort the words that end in the suffix -**tion**. Help students notice that this is the way most -**tion** words are spelled.

Sort rhymes:

| out | notion |
| scout | motion |

Reading Transfer: commotion, potion

Tell students, "Pretend you are reading and come to a new word." Have students put the words under the appropriate rhymes and use the rhymes to decode them.

Spelling Transfer: sprout, lotion

Tell students, "Pretend you are writing and need to spell each of these words." Have students tell you how each word begins. Then, have students find and use the appropriate rhymes to finish spelling each new word.

 ## Making Words Homework
See page 28 for complete Making Words Homework directions. See page 153 for a Making Words Homework reproducible. Send home the letters for **communications** home with students to make and remake words.

Word Detectives
See page 28 for complete Word Detectives directions. If the selected content-area word is **geothermal**, students might say the following words look like and sound like **geothermal**:

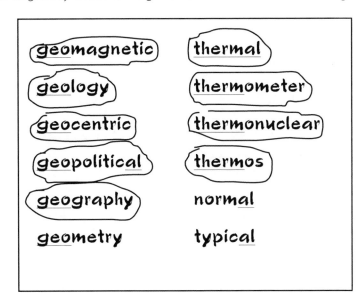

Underline the parts that look similar and circle the related words. Remind students that related words often help in determining the meaning of the chosen content word.

Word Detectives Homework

See page 30 for complete Word Detectives Homework directions. Type the words students generate in the Word Detectives lesson or use the reproducibles on pages 154 or 155 to record them.

Option 1: Have students sort the words, add category headings, and add any additional words they know.

Option 2: Have students write the root word for each word on the list that has a root word.

Goal Two: Word Wall Words

Continue to gather students' writing samples to determine which words will be introduced and placed on the Word Wall.

- Be sure to highlight what makes the words illogical or difficult to spell.

- Students need to chant and write each word as it is introduced, then check each word by chanting their spellings as they touch each letter.

- Post the new words on the Word Wall. Hold students accountable for spelling the posted words correctly in all of their writing.

Word Wall Review Activities

Review the Word Wall words throughout the week and month with the following activities.

Word Wall Riddles

See page 23 for complete directions for reviewing words using riddles.

Riddles focus students' attention on particular features of each word in a game-like activity. For example, if you have placed the word **terrible** on your Word Wall, your riddle might be, "Write the word that means the opposite of **terrific**."

Word Wall Be a Mind Reader

See page 47 for complete Word Wall Be a Mind Reader directions.

Select a word from the Word Wall. Give students five clues so that they can guess the word. For example, if you have added the word **favorite** to your Word Wall, you might use the following Be a Mind Reader lesson:

1. It is a word on the Word Wall.
2. It has more than two vowels.
3. It has more than one syllable.
4. The first two syllables spell the root of this word.
5. It fits in the sentence, "Vanilla is my _____ flavor of ice cream."

Goal Three: Visual Checking System

What Looks Right?

See page 33 for complete What Looks Right? directions.

trees	peas	freeze	please
disees	diseas	diseeze	disease
committees	committeas	committeeze	committease
oversees	overseas	overseeze	oversease
appees	appeas	appeeze	appease
guarantees	guaranteas	guaranteeze	guarantease
squees	squeas	squeeze	squease
pedigrees	pedigreas	pedigreeze	pedigrease
snees	sneas	sneeze	snease
chickpees	chickpeas	chickpeeze	chickpease
unees	uneas	uneeze	unease
retirees	retireas	retireeze	retirease
Yankees	Yankeas	Yankeeze	Yankease
antifrees	antifreas	antifreeze	antifrease
displees	displeas	displeeze	displease
unfrees	unfreas	unfreeze	unfrease
Frisbees®	Frisbeas	Frisbeeze	Frisbease
disees	diseas	diseeze	disease

Goal Four: Cross-Checking

Guess the Covered Word

See page 34 for complete Guess the Covered Word directions. Here is a possible Guess the Covered Word lesson from *Now Let Me Fly: The Story of a Slave Family* by Dolores Johnson (Sagebrush, 1999):

Slavery

From the mid-1500s to the mid-1800s, **millions** of African men, women, and children were taken forcibly from their homes and sold into slavery in the Americas. It is not known, even today, exactly how many millions died during the brutal capture, the forced march to the coast, or the agonizing **voyage** which brought them across the sea to this continent.

We all live with the **legacy** of slavery, even today. We must do all we can to insure that oppression of any group of people will never again be **tolerated**. We are all diminished when even one of us is not **free**.

January

Month at a Glance

January is here, and it is time to review your procedures. After the holidays, as with any break, students will need time to get back into the school routine. This means that you will need to remind them of your expectations. You may find that the amount of time for independent reading and writing must decrease until students rebuild their stamina. Word work continues as before and students continue to spend the majority of their time working with big words.

Here are the major things you will do during Working with Words in January to help students move toward meeting all four goals:

- **Goal One:** Polysyllabic Words

  Add seven more Nifty Thrifty Fifty words to the Word Wall. Use Be a Mind Reader, Riddles, and Mini-WORDO to review the words. Use the suggested Word Sort to extend the understanding of **-tion** and **-or** words and the Root Word lesson to focus on the word **music**. Use the Scavenger Hunt to review words with a suffix and a double consonant spelling change. Have students use the Nifty Thrifty Fifty Cards to explore combinations of prefixes, suffixes, and root words for all 36 words. Use the Making Words lesson to work with the suffix **-y**, the prefix **dis-**, and the root word **honest**. Use the Word Detectives lesson to help students use the prefixes and suffixes of content-area words to determine meanings.

- **Goal Two:** Word Wall Words

  Choose 8–10 more words from students' writing and add these to the Word Wall. Use spare minutes to review and practice all of the words through chanting and writing, Word Wall Riddles, and Be a Mind Reader activities. Hold students accountable for these words in all of their writing.

- **Goal Three:** Visual Checking System

  Use the What Looks Right? lesson to focus on the **oal**, **ole**, and **oll** patterns.

- **Goal Four:** Cross-Checking

  Use the Guess the Covered Word lessons to introduce content-area vocabulary or highlight a part of speech. This month, you might consider choosing excerpts from science texts.

Goal One: Polysyllabic Words

Nifty Thrifty Fifty Words

Introduce the following new words. See page 22 for directions for introducing Nifty Thrifty Fifty words.

dishonest: This is the root word **honest** with the prefix **dis-**. **Dis-** can signal an opposite. Other words with the prefix **dis-** include **disapprove**, **distasteful**, and **disobedient**.

illegal: This is the root word **legal** with the prefix **il-**. **Il-** signals an opposite. Similar words include **illogical** and **illegitimate**.

irresponsible: This is the root word **response** with the prefix **ir-** and the suffix **-ible**. **Ir-** signals an opposite relationship. The suffix **-ible** means "capable of or tending to." If you are **irresponsible**, you are unable to make the correct response or to take responsibility. Similar words include **irregular** and **irrational**. Other -ible words are **flexible** and **collectible**.

misunderstand: This is the root word **understand** with the prefix **mis-**. **Mis-** often signals an opposite relationship and also has a "bad" or "wrong" meaning, as in **mistake, misbehave,** and **miscount**.

performance: This is the root word **form** with the suffix -**ance** and the prefix **per-**. Another **per-** word is **perjury**. Other -**ance** words include **appearance, defiance,** and **resistance**.

rearrange: This is the root word **arrange** with the prefix **re-**. **Re-** often means "again." Other words in which **re-** means "again" include **redo, rewrite, reheat,** and **repaint**.

replacement: This is the root word **place** with the prefix **re-** and the suffix **-ment**. In this case, **re-** means "back." A **replacement** is something that is used in place of something else. Similar words are **rewind, recall,** and **recycle**.

Nifty Thrifty Fifty Review Activities
Nifty Thrifty Fifty Be a Mind Reader
See page 47 for complete Be a Mind Reader directions.

1. It is a Nifty Thrifty Fifty word.
2. It has a prefix and a suffix.
3. The prefix means "opposite."
4. It has four syllables. (independence, discovery)
5. It begins with a **d**. (discovery)

1. It is a Nifty Thrifty Fifty word.
2. It is an adjective, or describing word.
3. It only has a suffix.
4. It has two syllables. (hopeless, richest)
5. Its suffix means "the most." (richest)

1. It is a Nifty Thrifty Fifty word.
2. It only has a suffix.
3. It has fewer than 10 letters.
4. It has two syllables. (hopeless, swimming, richest)
5. The final consonant of the root word is doubled before adding the suffix. (swimming)

1. It is a Nifty Thrifty Fifty word.
2. It has four syllables.
3. It has a prefix and a suffix.
4. It begins with a **c**. (communities, continuous, conversation, community)
5. It fits in the sentence, "When the man everyone thought had died entered the room, all _____ stopped." (conversation)

1. It is a Nifty Thrifty Fifty word.
2. It has four syllables.
3. It has a prefix and a suffix.
4. It starts with a vowel. (encouragement, independence)
5. It fits in the sentence, "America fought for its _____ from England." (independence)

1. It is a Nifty Thrifty Fifty word.
2. It has four vowels.
3. It has three syllables.
4. It is a noun. (musician, submarine)
5. It has the same suffix as **beautician** and **magician**. (musician)

1. It is a Nifty Thrifty Fifty word.
2. It has a prefix and a suffix.
3. It has a spelling change.
4. It begins with a **c**. (composer, community, communities, conversation)
5. It is a plural, or means more than one of something. (communities)

Nifty Thrifty Fifty Riddles

Have each student number a piece of paper to correspond with the number of words you have time to review. Give the following clues for the new Nifty Thrifty Fifty words introduced this month.

1. Write the word with the same prefix as **discovery**. (dishonest)

2. Write the word with only a prefix that means "to do again." (rearrange)

3. Write the three-syllable word with a prefix that means "opposite." (illegal)

4. Write the four-syllable word. (misunderstand)

5. Write the word that means "not responsible." (irresponsible)

6. A show or a concert could be called a _____. (performance)

7. Write the word that has the prefix **re**- the suffix -**ment**. (replacement)

Have each student check his own paper by chanting the letters in each word aloud again and underlining each letter as he says it.

Nifty Thrifty Fifty Mini-WORDO

See page 37 for complete Mini-WORDO directions.

Have students write the following Nifty Thrifty Fifty words on their blank Mini-WORDO card:

irresponsible	performance	rearrange
misunderstand	illegal	transportation
dishonest	replacement	unfriendly

Possible combined words to show and say:

misplaced	responsible	legally	irreplaceable
displacement	reform	understanding	transform

Beyond Nifty Thrifty Fifty

Nifty Thrifty Fifty Cards

See page 24 for directions for using Nifty Thrifty Fifty Cards to make new words. Students should write the following morphemes on individual cards:

prefix	root	suffix
*dis-	honest	
il-	legal	
ir-	response	-ible
mis-	understand	
per-	form	-ance
re-	arrange	
*re-	place	*-ment

*These morpheme cards were made for a previous word.

Words to make: displacement, uniformed

Ask students to make their own words from the morphemes.

Neologism to make: misformable

Ask a student to use the neologism in a sensible sentence. Be sure the sentence defines the word as "something you are able to form incorrectly." For example, "Without assembly directions, the new bike was misformable."

Ask students to make their own neologisms. Suggest that they make up riddles or say sentences that will help other students discover the spelling and meaning of their neologisms.

January

Nifty Thrifty Fifty Cards Homework

See page 25 for complete Nifty Thrifty Fifty Cards Homework directions. Have each student take home the January Morpheme chart (page 137) to make two additional words and one additional neologism. Have students write riddles or defining sentences for their neologisms.

Word Sorts

Root Word Lesson: music

(from the Nifty Thrifty Fifty word **musician**, introduced in August/September)

See page 42 for complete Root Word Lesson directions.

Definition: sounds, usually produced by instruments or voices, which are arranged or played in order to crate a pleasing or stimulating effect

Write these words:

music   nonmusical

Students might suggest:

musician   musical   musically

Prefix and Suffix Sorts

See page 39 for complete Prefix and Suffix Sorts directions.

Suffix Sort: -tion

(from the Nifty Thrifty Fifty word **conversation**, introduced in December)

-tion (suffix)	spelling/pronunciation only

See page 144 for a reproducible of this suffix sort. To introduce this sort you might say, **"Conversation** is the word **converse** with the suffix -**ation** added and the **e** dropped, so **conversation** fits in the first column. **Nation** ends with **a-t-i-o-n**, but **n** is not a root word, so **nation** fits in the second column."

Show and say the following words one at a time and have students put each word in the correct column:

vacation   plantation   formation   carnation   donation   motion

portion   flotation   pollution   action   station

-tion (suffix)	spelling/pronunciation only
conversation	nation
vacation	plantation
formation	carnation
donation	motion
flotation	portion
pollution	station
action	

Suffix Sort: -or

(from the Nifty Thrifty Fifty word **governor**, introduced in October)

-or (suffix) someone or something who does	spelling/pronunciation only

See page 145 for a reproducible of this suffix sort. To introduce this sort you might say, "**Governor** is the root word **govern** with the suffix -**or**. Like -**er**, the suffix -**or** often signifies a person or thing that does something, so **governor** fits in the first column. **Favor** ends with **o-r** but **fav** isn't a root word, so **favor** fits in the second column."

Show and say the following words one at a time and have students put each word in the correct column:

color	actor	estimator	scissor	humor	editor	advisor
visitor	razor	corridor	vapor	divisor	anchor	director
donator	rotator	flavor	tormentor	harbor	counselor	labor
projector	confessor	predictor	tumor	decorator	escalator	meteor
splendor						

-or (suffix) someone or something who does	spelling/pronunciation only
governor	favor
actor	color
estimator	scissor
editor	humor
advisor	razor
visitor	corridor
divisor	vapor
director	anchor
donator	flavor
rotator	harbor
tormentor	labor
counselor	meteor
projector	tumor
confessor	splendor
predictor	
decorator	
escalator	

Scavenger Hunt

See page 42 for complete Scavenger Hunt directions.

The suggested hunt for January is for words that have a suffix and a doubled consonant spelling change. If a student reads *Earthquakes* by Deborah Heiligman (Scholastic Reference, 2003), he might add the following words to the Scavenger Hunt chart:

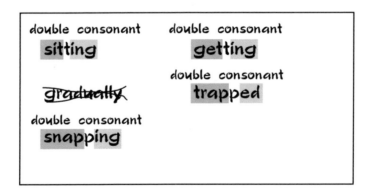

Use two different colors of markers or highlighters to identify the root and prefix of each word on the chart. If there is a spelling change, write what changed above the root. Cross off any word students agree does not have a suffix and a doubled consonant spelling change.

Scavenger Hunt Homework

See page 44 for complete Scavenger Hunt Homework directions. Have each student find three or more words that fit this week's hunt. Here is an example using *Alexander, Who Used to Be Rich Last Sunday* by Judith Viorst (Scholastic, 1978):

Alexander, Who Used to Be Rich Last Sunday by Judith Viorst
✓ called
✓ kidding
~~especially~~
✓ sitting

Making Words

See page 25 for complete Making Words directions.

dishonesty

Letters: e i o d h n s s t y

Make Words: dine, hose, nose, noise, noisy, shine, shiny, honest, honesty, destiny/density, dishonest, dishonesty

Directions:

• Tell students how many letters to use to make each word.

• Emphasize how changing just one letter or rearranging letters makes a different word.

> "Add a letter to **honest** to spell **honesty**."

> "Change one letter in **noise** to spell **noisy**."

> "Use the same letters in **destiny** to spell **density**."

• When students are not just adding or changing one letter, cue them to start over.

> "Start over and use nine letters to spell **dishonest**."

• Give meaning or sentence clues when needed to clarify the word they are making.

> "Start over and use seven letters to spell **destiny**. 'It was Nelson Mandela's **destiny** to bring down the system of apartheid in South Africa.'"

• Give students one minute to figure out the secret word, then give clues if needed.

> "Our secret word is related to the word **honest**."

Sort: Sort related words and use sentence clues to show how they are related.

noise, noisy

> "When there is a lot of **noise**, we say it is very **noisy**."

shine, shiny

> "Something that has a **shine** is **shiny**."

honest, honesty, dishonest, dishonesty

"The people were **honest** and hardworking. Everyone respected them for their **honesty**."

"**Dishonest** is the opposite of **honest**. **Dishonesty** is the opposite of **honesty**."

Sort rhymes:

dine	**nose**
shine	**hose**

Reading Transfer: borderline, valentine

Tell students, "Pretend you are reading and come to a new word." Have students put the words under the appropriate rhymes and use the rhymes to decode them.

Spelling Transfer: outline, dispose

Tell students, "Pretend you are writing and need to spell each of these words." Have students tell you how each word begins. Then, have students find and use the appropriate rhymes to finish spelling each new word.

Making Words Homework

See page 28 for complete Making Words Homework directions. See page 153 for a Making Words Homework reproducible. Send home the letters for **dishonesty** with students to make and remake words.

Word Detectives

See page 28 for complete Word Detectives directions.

If the selected content-area word is **constitutional**, students might say the following words look like and sound like **constitutional**:

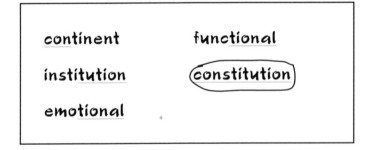

Underline the parts that look similar and circle the related words. Remind students that related words often help in determining the meaning of the chosen content word.

Word Detectives Homework

See page 30 for complete Word Detectives Homework directions. Type the words students generate in the Word Detectives lesson or use the reproducibles on pages 154 or 155 to record them.

Option 1: Have students sort the words, add category headings, and add any additional words they know.

Option 2: Have students write the root word for each word on the list that has a root word.

Goal Two: Word Wall Words

Continue to gather students' writing samples to determine which words will be introduced and placed on the Word Wall.

- Be sure to highlight what makes the words illogical or difficult to spell.

- Students need to chant and write each word as it is introduced, then check each word by chanting their spellings as they touch each letter.

- Post the new words on the Word Wall. Hold students accountable for spelling the posted words correctly in all of their writing.

Word Wall Review Activities

Review the Word Wall words throughout the week and month with the following activities.

Word Wall Riddles

See page 23 for complete directions for reviewing words using riddles.

Riddles focus students on particular features of each word in a game-like activity. For example, if you have placed the words **a lot** on your Word Wall, your riddle might be, "Write the words that complete the sentence, 'I don't want a little ice cream; I want _____ of ice cream.'"

Word Wall Be a Mind Reader

See page 47 for complete Be a Mind Reader directions.

Select a word from the Word Wall. Give students five clues so that they can guess the word. For example, if you have added the word **know** to your Word Wall, you might use the following Be a Mind Reader lesson:

1. It is a word on the Word Wall.
2. It is a four-letter word.
3. It is a homophone.
4. It has one syllable.
5. It rhymes with **show**.

Goal Three: Visual Checking System

What Looks Right?

See page 33 for complete What Looks Right? directions.

goal	hole	toll
unroal	unrole	unroll
enroal	enrole	enroll
consoal	console	consoll
bedroal	bedrole	bedroll
tadpoal	tadpole	tadpoll
subgoal	subgole	subgoll
charcoal	charcole	charcoll
porthoal	porthole	portholl
loophoal	loophole	loopholl
camisoal	camisole	camisoll
steamroal	steamrole	steamroll

Goal Four: Cross-Checking

Guess the Covered Word

See page 34 for complete Guess the Covered Word directions. Here is a possible Guess the Covered Word lesson adapted from *Everything You Need to Know About Science Homework* by Anne Zeman and Kate Kelly (Scholastic Reference, 2005):

Overpopulation

Overpopulation occurs when there are not enough resources for plants, animals, or people to **survive**. Without enough **resources**, plants or animals may become endangered or extinct. When too many people live in one place there may not be enough **housing**. Safe food and water may be **scarce**. Too many animals or people living in a small space may mean more **disease**, fighting, and starvation.

February

Month at a Glance

By February, your students should be very comfortable with the activities in the Working with Words Block. Many of them will have their favorites, but more importantly, you should hear more "word" talk. Are students using the strategies they have learned in the activities? Are they applying the patterns and the morphemes to new words they encounter in their reading and writing? This is the time of year that transfer should be in frequent use.

Here are the major things you will do during Working with Words in February to help students move toward meeting all four goals:

- **Goal One:** Polysyllabic Words

  Add seven more Nifty Thrifty Fifty words to the Word Wall. Use Be a Mind Reader, Riddles, and Mini-WORDO to review the words. Use the suggested Word Sort to extend the understanding of the suffix -**ous** and the prefix **re**-. Use the Root Word lesson to focus on the root word **govern**. Use the Scavenger Hunt to review **re**- words. Have students use the Nifty Thrifty Fifty Cards to explore combinations of prefixes, suffixes, and root words for all 43 words. Use the Making Words lesson to work with the suffix -**ion**, the prefix **ex**-, and the root word **express**. Use the Word Detectives lesson to help students use the prefixes and suffixes of content-area words to determine meanings.

- **Goal Two:** Word Wall Words

  Choose 8–10 more words from students' writing and add them to the Word Wall. Use spare minutes to review and practice all of the words through chanting and writing, Word Wall Riddles, and Be a Mind Reader activities. Hold students accountable for these words in all of their writing.

- **Goal Three:** Visual Checking System

  Use the What Looks Right? lesson to focus on the **oan**, **one**, and **own** patterns.

- **Goal Four:** Cross-Checking

  Use the Guess the Covered Word lessons to introduce content-area vocabulary or highlight a part of speech. This month, you might consider choosing a book review.

Goal One: Polysyllabic Words

Nifty Thrifty Fifty Words

Introduce the following new words. See page 22 for directions for introducing Nifty Thrifty Fifty words.

deodorize: This is the root word **odor** with the prefix **de**- and the suffix -**ize**. The prefix **de**- means "down or away," and the suffix -**ize** means "to make." When you **deodorize** something, you take away the odor. Other examples in which **de**- means "down or away" include **deflate**, **defrost**, and **debug**. Other words with -**ize** include **personalize** and **computerize**. When the prefix **de**- meaning "down or away" is added to **personalize**, it becomes **depersonalize**.

different: Different is the root **differ** with the suffix -**ent**. When things differ, they are **different**. Similar words are **dependent** and **excellent**. When people depend on you, we say they are **dependent**. When you excel at something, you are **excellent**.

employee: Employee is the root word **employ** with the suffix -**ee** added. The suffix -**ee** means "person who." A person who is nominated for president is a **nominee**. A person being trained is a **trainee**. The people who are evacuated during a hurricane are **evacuees**.

international: International is the root word **nation** with the prefix **inter-** and the suffix -**al**. Inter- often means "between" as in **intersection** and **Internet**. Other words with the -**al** suffix include **natural** and **accidental**. Notice how the pronunciation changes when **nation** becomes **national**.

invasion: Invasion is the word **invade** with the -**sion** suffix. The spelling and pronunciation change is common for many words ending in -**de**, such as **provide/provision**, **collide/collision**, and **erode/erosion**. Things you provide are **provisions**. When two trains collide, it is a **collision**. When the earth erodes, it is **erosion**.

prehistoric: This is the root word **history** with the prefix **pre-** and the suffix -**ic**. The prefix **pre-** means "before." Nothing could happen before history, but **prehistoric** means it happened before history was written down. Thus, dinosaurs are prehistoric creatures. There are many other words in which the prefix **pre-** means "before," including **prefix**, **preview**, and **precaution**. Other words with -**ic** include **poetic** and **allergic**.

signature: This is the root word **sign** with the suffix -**ature** (-**ure**). In some words, you will see only the letters -**ure**. Another example of the -**ature** suffix is **curvature**, which means "the curving of." Examples with the -**ure** suffix include **pleasure** (**please**) and **legislature** (**legislate**). In **signature**, the process of signing, there is also a pronunciation change. Similar changes happen in the related words **signal**, **signify**, and **significance**.

Nifty Thrifty Fifty Review Activities
Nifty Thrifty Fifty Be a Mind Reader
See page 47 for complete Be a Mind Reader directions.

1. It is a Nifty Thrifty Fifty word.
2. It has at least nine letters.
3. The suffix changes a **y** to **i** before being added.
4. It has three syllables. (beautiful, happiness)
5. The root word is **beauty**. (beautiful)

1. It is a Nifty Thrifty Fifty word.
2. It has a prefix and a suffix.
3. It has three or more syllables.
4. The suffix is -**ment**. (encouragement, replacement)
5. A synonym might be **substitute**. (replacement)

1. It is a Nifty Thrifty Fifty word.
2. It has a prefix and a suffix.
3. It has three syllables.
4. The root word drops the **e** before adding the suffix. (composer, expensive, nonliving)
5. It begins with an **n**. (nonliving)

1. It is a Nifty Thrifty Fifty word.
2. Its prefix means "opposite."
3. It has three syllables.
4. It is an adjective, or describing word. (dishonest, illegal, unfinished, unfriendly, unpleasant)
5. It fits in the sentence, "It is _____ to drive faster than the speed limit." (illegal)

1. It is a Nifty Thrifty Fifty word.
2. Its prefix means "opposite."
3. It has three syllables.
4. It is an adjective, or describing word. (dishonest, illegal, unfinished, unfriendly, unpleasant)
5. It means "the opposite of **pleasant**." (unpleasant)

1. It is a Nifty Thrifty Fifty word.
2. It has three syllables.
3. It has a prefix and a suffix.
4. It begins with a vowel. (impression, unfriendly, unfinished, unpleasant)
5. It has the root word **press**. (impression)

1. It is a Nifty Thrifty Fifty word.
2. It does not have an **i** in it.
3. It has three syllables.
4. It has a prefix and a suffix. (replacement, performance, unpleasant, composer)
5. It begins with a **p**. (performance)

Nifty Thrifty Fifty Riddles

See page 23 for complete directions for using riddles to review words.

Have each student number a piece of paper to correspond with the number of words you have time to review. Give the following clues for the new Nifty Thrifty Fifty words introduced this month.

1. Write the word with a prefix that means "between or among." (international)
2. This word is a synonym for **dissimilar**. (different)
3. Write the word that means "before history was written." (prehistoric)
4. This word is a synonym for **attack**. (invasion)
5. Write the word that means "a person who is employed." (employee)

6.   This word means "to take the smell away." (deodorize)

7.   This word is the result of signing. (signature)

Have each student check her own paper by chanting the letters in each word aloud again and underlining each letter as she says it.

Nifty Thrifty Fifty Mini-WORDO

See page 37 for complete Mini-WORDO directions.

Have students write the following Nifty Thrifty Fifty words on their blank Mini-WORDO cards:

independence	illegal	different
richest	deodorize	international
prettier	employee	valuable

Possible combined words to show and say:

employable	legalize	deodorizer	interdependent
invaluable	nationalize	difference	richer
prettiest			

Beyond Nifty Thrifty Fifty
Nifty Thrifty Fifty Cards

See page 24 for complete directions for using Nifty Thrifty Fifty Cards to make new words.

Students should write the following morphemes on individual cards:

prefix	root	suffix
de-	odor	-ize
	differ	-ent
em-	employ	-ee
inter-	nation	-al
*in-	invade	-sion
pre-	history	-ic
	sign	-ature

*These morpheme cards were made for a previous word.

Words to make: signal, internationalization

Ask students to make their own words from the morphemes.

Neologism to make: interhistorian

Ask a student to use the neologism in a sensible sentence. Be sure the sentence defines the word as "someone who studies between historical times." For example, "He is an interhistorian for the 18th century and the 21st century."

Ask students to make their own neologisms. Suggest that they make up riddles or say sentences that will help other students discover the spelling and meaning of their neologisms.

Nifty Thrifty Fifty Cards Homework

See page 25 for complete directions for Nifty Thrifty Fifty Cards Homework. Have each student take home the February Morpheme chart (page 138) to make two additional words and one additional neologism. Have students write riddles or defining sentences for their neologisms.

Word Sorts

See page 39 for complete Prefix and Suffix Sorts directions.

Suffix Sort: -ous

(from the Nifty Thrifty Fifty word **continuous**, introduced in December)

-ous (suffix) full of	spelling/pronunciation only

See page 146 for a reproducible of this suffix sort. To introduce this sort you might say, "**Continuous** is the root word **continue** with the suffix -**ous** and the **e** dropped. The suffix -**ous** means 'full of.' **Continuous** fits in the first column. **Obnoxious** ends in **o-u-s**, but **obnoxi** isn't a word, so **obnoxious** fits in the second column."

Show and say the following words one a time and have students put each word in the correct column:

hideous	spacious	joyous	tremendous	vicious	nervous	serious
ferocious	wondrous	gracious	anxious	cautious	precious	famous

-ous (suffix) full of	spelling/pronunciation only
continuous	obnoxious
spacious	hideous
joyous	tremendous
nervous	vicious
wondrous	ferocious
gracious	anxious
famous	precious
cautious	serious

Prefix Sort: re-

(from the Nifty Thrifty Fifty words **rearrange** and **replacement**, introduced in January)

re- (prefix) back or again	spelling/pronunciation only	part of the word/ different pronunciation

See page 146 for a reproducible of this prefix sort. To introduce this sort you might say, "**Rearrange** is the root word **arrange** with the prefix **re**-, meaning 'again.' **Replacement** is the root word **place** with the prefix **re**-, meaning 'back.' A **replacement** is something that is put back in place of something else. **Rearrange** and **replacement** fit in the first column. **Resort** begins with **r-e**, but **resort** doesn't mean 'to sort again,' so **resort** fits in the second column. **Rectangular** begins with **r-e**, but **ctangular** isn't a word. The **r-e** in **rectangular** doesn't sound like the **r-e** in **rearrange**, so **rectangular** fits in the third column."

Show and say the following words one at a time and have students put each word in the correct column:

research	region	republic	reptile	repay	regular	relocate
reindeer	respect	recline	reunite	reunion	recital	relative
relaxation	reliable					

re- (prefix) back or again	spelling/pronunciation only	part of the word/ different pronunciation
rearrange	resort	rectangular
replacement	region	reptile
research	republic	regular
repay	respect	reindeer
relocate	recline	relative
reunite	recital	
reunion	relaxation	
	reliable	

Root Word Lesson: govern

(from the Nifty Thrifty Fifty word **governor**, introduced in October)

See page 42 for complete Root Word Lesson directions.

Definition: to have political authority; to be responsible officially for directing the affairs, policies, and economy of a state, country, or organization

Write these words:

governor   misgoverned   governess

Students might suggest:

government   governed   governing   governable   antigovernment

governs   nongovernmental   intergovernmental

Scavenger Hunt

See page 42 for complete Scavenger Hunt directions.

The suggested hunt for February is for words that begin with the prefix **re**-. If a student reads *Freedom Train: The Story of Harriet Tubman* by Dorothy Sterling (Scholastic, 1987), he might add the following **re**- words to the Scavenger Hunt chart:

removed

returned

February

Use two different colors of markers or highlighters to identify the root and suffix of each word on the chart. If there is a spelling change, write what changed above the root. Cross off any word students agree does not have the prefix **re**-

Bats
by Lisa deMauro
~~ready~~
✓return
~~reason~~
✓research
~~read~~
✓react
✓reorganize

Scavenger Hunt Homework

See page 44 for complete Scavenger Hunt Homework directions. Have each student find three or more words that fit this month's hunt. Here is an example using *Bats* by Lisa deMauro (Parachute Press, Inc., 1990):

Making Words

See page 25 for complete Making Words directions.

expression
Letters: e e i o n p r s s x

Make Words: sore/rose, pose, open, ripe, ripen, snore, press, reopen/opener, expose, expire, express, ripeness, expression

Directions:

- Tell students how many letters to use to make each word.
- Emphasize how changing just one letter or rearranging letters makes a different word.

  "Add a letter to **ripe** to spell **ripen**."

  "Change one letter in **rose** to spell **pose**."

  "Use the same letters in **reopen** to spell **opener**."
- When students are not just adding or changing one letter, cue them to start over.

  "Start over and use eight letters to spell **ripeness**."
- Give meaning or sentence clues when needed to clarify the word they are making.

  "Start over and use six letters to spell **expire**. 'We bought our truck on Saturday because the special offer was about to **expire**.'"
- Give students one minute to figure out the secret word, then give clues if needed.

  "Our secret word is related to the word **express**."

Sort: Sort related words and use sentence clues to show how they are related.

press, **express**, **expression**

"The word **express** means to 'press out.' When you **express** your feelings, you **press** those feelings out. We can tell how you feel by your facial **expression**."

ripe, ripen, ripeness

"We watched the peaches **ripen** and picked them when they were perfectly **ripe**. Their **ripeness** gave them a wonderful sweetness."

open, opener, reopen

"We use a can **opener** to **open** cans. **Reopen** means 'to open again.'"

Sort rhymes:

snore	rose	press
sore	pose	ripeness
	expose	

Reading Transfer: distress, recess

Tell students, "Pretend you are reading and come to a new word." Have students put the words under the appropriate rhymes and use the rhymes to decode them.

Spelling Transfer: confess, explore

Tell students, "Pretend you are writing and need to spell each of these words." Have them tell you how each word begins. Then, have students find and use the appropriate rhymes to finish spelling each new word.

Making Words Homework

See page 28 for complete Making Words Homework directions. See page 153 for a Making Words Homework reproducible. Send the letters for **expression** home with students to make and remake words.

Word Detectives

See page 28 for complete Word Detectives directions. If the selected content word is **circumference**, students might say the following words look like and sound like **circumference**:

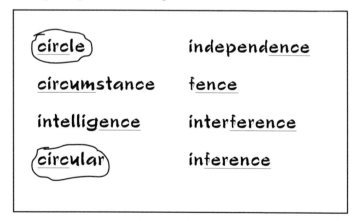

Underline the parts that look similar and circle the related words. Remind students that related words often help in determining the meaning of the chosen content word.

February

Word Detectives Homework

See page 30 for complete Word Detectives Homework directions. Type the words students generate in the Word Detectives lesson or use the reproducibles on pages 154 or 155 to record them.

Option 1: Have students sort the words, add category headings, and add any additional words they know.

Option 2: Have students write the root word for each word on the list that has a root word.

Goal Two: Word Wall Words

Continue to gather students' writing samples to determine which words will be introduced and placed on the Word Wall.

- Be sure to highlight what makes the words illogical or difficult to spell.

- Students need to chant and write each word as it is introduced, then check each word by chanting their spellings as they touch each letter.

- Post the new words on the Word Wall. Hold students accountable for spelling the posted words correctly in all of their writing.

Word Wall Review Activities

Review Word Wall words throughout the week and month with the following activities.

Word Wall Riddles

See page 23 for complete directions for reviewing words using riddles.

Riddles focus students on particular features of each word in a game-like activity. For example, if you have placed the word **what** on your Word Wall, your riddle might be, "Write the word that should rhyme with **hat**, but rhymes with **hot**."

Word Wall Be a Mind Reader

See page 47 for complete Be a Mind Reader directions.

Select a word from the Word Wall. Give students five clues so that they can guess the word. For example, if you have added the word **because** to your Word Wall, you might use the following Be a Mind Reader lesson:

1. It is a word on the Word Wall.
2. It has two syllables.
3. It has more than two vowels.
4. It has more than five letters.
5. It begins with a **b**.

Goal Three: Visual Checking System

What Looks Right?

See page 33 for complete What Looks Right? directions.

moan	phone	own
bemoan	bemone	bemown
disoan	disone	disown
unknoan	unknone	unknown
monotoan	monotone	monotown
milestoan	milestone	milestown
tromboan	trombone	trombown
overgroan	overgrone	overgrown
telephoan	telephone	telephown
saxophoan	saxophone	saxophown
handbloan	handblone	handblown
microphoan	microphone	microphown

Goal Four: Cross-Checking

Guess the Covered Word

See page 34 for complete Guess the Covered Word directions. Here is a possible Guess the Covered Word lesson from a Barnes and Noble online review of the Roald Dahl book, *Boy: Tales of Childhood* (Puffin, 1999):

Parts of Speech: Adjectives

A Book Review of *Boy*

Boy is the **charming** autobiography of Roald Dahl. Writing about many of his boyhood adventures, the author recalls only those that stand out as **spectacular**. There are **humorous** incidents. There are **sad** events. The most **surprising** thing is that they are all true.

March

Month at a Glance

Spring is approaching and the end of school is near. March is the last month for new Nifty Thrifty Fifty words, but Word Wall selections will continue. After the last of the 50 words are added, use the remainder of the school year to review and apply what has been learned.

Here are the major things you will do during Working with Words in March to help students move toward meeting all four goals:

- **Goal One:** Polysyllabic Words

  Add the last seven Nifty Thrifty Fifty words to the Word Wall. Use Be a Mind Reader, Riddles, and Mini-WORDO to review the words. Use the suggested Word Sort to extend the understanding of the prefix **ir-** and the suffix **-en**. Use the Scavenger Hunt to review words that begin with the prefixes **in-** (meaning "in"), **in-** (meaning "not,"), and **inter-**. Have students use the Nifty Thrifty Fifty Cards to explore combinations of prefixes, suffixes, and root words for all 50 words. Use the Making Words lesson to work with the suffix **-ing**, the prefix **sub-**, and the root word **freeze**. Use the Word Detectives lesson to help students use the prefixes and suffixes of content-area words to determine meanings.

- **Goal Two:** Word Wall Words

  Choose 8–10 more words from students' writing and add them to the Word Wall. Use spare minutes to review and practice all of the words through chanting and writing, Word Wall Riddles, and Be a Mind Reader activities. Hold students accountable for these words in all of their writing.

- **Goal Three:** Visual Checking System

  Use the What Looks Right? lesson to focus on the **air**, **are**, and **ear** patterns.

- **Goal Four:** Cross-Checking

  Use Guess the Covered Word lessons to introduce content-area vocabulary or highlight a part of speech. This month, you might consider choosing excerpts from social studies texts.

Goal One: Polysyllabic Words

Nifty Thrifty Fifty Words

Introduce the following new words. See page 22 for complete directions for introducing Nifty Thrifty Fifty words.

antifreeze: This is the root word **freeze** with the prefix **anti-**, which means "against." Other words in which **anti-** means "against" include **antislavery**, **antibody**, and **antisocial**.

forecast: This is the root word **cast** with the prefix **fore**-, meaning "before" or "in front of." Other words in which **fore**- has one of these meanings include **forehead**, **foresight**, **foreshadow**, and **forewarn**.

midnight: This is the word **night** with the prefix **mid**-, meaning "middle." Other words in which **mid**- has this meaning include **midpoint**, **midlife**, **midyear**, and **midair**.

overpower: This is the root word **power** with the prefix **over**-, meaning "more than" or "too much." Other words in which **over**- has this meaning include **overcharge**, **overflow**, **overjoyed**, and **overload**.

semifinal: This is the root word **final** with the prefix **semi**-, meaning "half." Other words in which **semi**- has this meaning include **semicolon**, **semiannual**, and **semisweet**.

supermarkets: This is the word **market** with the prefix **super**-, meaning "really big," and the suffix -**s**, meaning "more than one," or plural. Other words in which **super**- has this meaning include **superpower**, **supermodel**, and **superman**.

underweight: This is the root word **weight** with the prefix **under**-, meaning "below." Other words in which **under**- has one of these meanings include **underclass**, **underground**, and **undertow**.

Nifty Thrifty Fifty Review Activities
Nifty Thrifty Fifty Be a Mind Reader
See page 47 for complete Be a Mind Reader directions.

1. It is a Nifty Thrifty Fifty word.
2. It has four syllables.
3. It has four vowels.
4. It only has a prefix. (impossible, misunderstand, overpower, semifinal)
5. The prefix means "not or wrong." (misunderstand)

1. It is a Nifty Thrifty Fifty word.
2. It has a prefix.
3. It has three syllables.
4. It has four vowels. (rearrange, submarine, underweight)
5. The prefix means "to do something again." (rearrange)

1. It is a Nifty Thrifty Fifty word.
2. There are four words listed under the beginning letter.
3. It has three syllables.
4. It is an adjective, or describing word. (dishonest, different, expensive)
5. It means "the opposite of **cheap**." (expensive)

1. It is a Nifty Thrifty Fifty word.
2. It has four syllables.
3. It has a prefix and a suffix.
4. It has a spelling change. (communities, continuous, conversation)
5. It means "never ending." (continuous)

1. It is a Nifty Thrifty Fifty word.
2. It is a singular noun.
3. It has a prefix and a suffix.
4. It has less than 10 letters. (composer, community, employee)
5. It has four syllables. (community)

1. It is a Nifty Thrifty Fifty word.
2. It has three syllables.
3. It is the only word listed under the beginning letter.
4. It has five vowels. (antifreeze, beautiful)
5. The prefix means "the opposite of." (antifreeze)

1. It is a Nifty Thrifty Fifty word.
2. It begins with the letters **u-n**.
3. It has three syllables.
4. It has a prefix. (underweight, unfinished, unfriendly, unpleasant)
5. The prefix means "below or less than." (underweight)

1. It is a Nifty Thrifty Fifty word.
2. It has four syllables.
3. It doesn't have a suffix.
4. It has nine letters. (community, overpower, semifinal)
5. It can mean "the sporting event that occurs just before the final event." (semifinal)

Nifty Thrifty Fifty Riddles

See page 23 for complete directions for using riddles to review words.

Have each student number a piece of paper to correspond with the number of words you have time to review. Give the following clues for the new Nifty Thrifty Fifty words introduced this month.

1. This word means "not heavy enough." (underweight)
2. Write the word that means "the next to last round in a tournament." (semifinal)
3. This word is a synonym for **predict**. (forecast)
4. Write the word that is a synonym for the neologism semievening. (midnight)
5. This is the word for really big grocery stores. (supermarkets)
6. Write the word with the prefix that means "against" and no suffix. (antifreeze)
7. This is an antonym for **defeat**. (overpower)

Have each student check his own paper by chanting the letters in each word aloud again and underlining each letter as he says it.

Nifty Thrifty Fifty Mini-WORDO

See page 37 for complete Mini-WORDO directions.

Have students write the following Nifty Thrifty Fifty words on their blank Mini-WORDO cards:

hopeless	international	replacement	underweight
musician	prehistoric	signature	continuous
dishonest			

Possible combined words to show and say:

undersign	discontinue	consignment	historian
weightless	musical	signal	continual

Beyond Nifty Thrifty Fifty

Nifty Thrifty Fifty Cards

See page 24 for complete directions for using Nifty Thrifty Fifty Cards to make new words.

Students should write the following morphemes on individual cards:

prefix	root	suffix
anti-	freeze	
fore-	cast	
mid-	night	
semi-	final	
over-	power	
super-	market	-s
under-	weight	

Words to make: overcast, invasiveness

Ask students to make their own words from the morphemes.

Neologism to make: forelegalize

Ask a student to use the neologism in a sensible sentence. Be sure the sentence defines the word as "to legalize something before it becomes illegal." For example, "The governor of Missouri decided to forelegalize owning a pet alligator."

Ask students to make their own neologisms. Suggest that they make up riddles or say sentences that will help other students discover the spelling and meaning of their neologisms.

Nifty Thrifty Fifty Cards Homework

See page 25 for complete Nifty Thrifty Fifty Cards Homework directions. Have each student take home the March Morpheme chart (pages 139–140) to make two additional words and one additional neologism. Have students write riddles or defining sentences for their neologisms.

Word Sorts

See page 39 for complete Prefix and Suffix Sorts directions.

Prefix Sort: ir-

(from the Nifty Thrifty Fifty word **irresponsible**, introduced in January)

ir- (prefix) opposite	spelling/pronunciation only	part of the word/ different pronunciation

See page 147 for a reproducible of this prefix sort. To introduce this sort you might say, "**Irresponsible** is the word **response** with the prefix **ir-** and the suffix **-ible**. **Ir-** signals an opposite relationship. If you are **irresponsible**, you are unable to make the correct response or to be responsible. **Irresponsible** fits in the first column. **Irrigate** begins with **i-r** but **rigate** isn't a root word, so **irrigate** fits in the second column. **Iranian** begins with **I-r** but **anian** isn't a word and the **I-r** doesn't sound like the **i-r** in **irresponsible**, so **Iranian** belongs in the last column."

Show and say the following words one at a time and have students put each word in the correct column:

irate   irrational   irritable   irregular   iris

irresistible   iron   irruption   irreversible   ironic

ir- (prefix) opposite	spelling/pronunciation only	part of the word/ different pronunciation
irresponsible	irrigate	Iranian
irrational	irritable	irate
irregular	irruption	iris
irresistible		iron
irreversible		ironic

Suffix Sort: -en

(from the Nifty Thrifty Fifty word **forgotten**, introduced in December)

-en (suffix) cause to be or have	spelling/pronunciation only

See page 147 for a reproducible of this suffix sort. To introduce this sort you might say, "**Forgotten** is the root word **forgot** with the suffix -**en** and the **t** doubled. The suffix -**en** means 'cause to be or have.' **Forgotten** fits in the first column. **Amen** ends with **e-n** but **am** isn't the root word for **amen**, so the word fits in the second column."

Show and say the following words one at a time and have students put each word in the correct column:

hidden	abdomen	alien	driven	mistaken	unwritten	women
freshmen	unbroken	outspoken	oven	kitchen	given	siren
linen	taken	unbeaten	mitten	pollen	seven	dozen

-en (suffix) cause to be or have	spelling/pronunciation only
forgotten	amen
hidden	abdomen
driven	alien
mistaken	dozen
unwritten	freshmen
unbroken	women
outspoken	kitchen
given	siren
taken	linen
unbeaten	mitten
	oven
	pollen
	seven

March

Scavenger Hunt

See page 42 for complete Scavenger Hunt directions.

The suggested hunt for March is for words that begin with the prefixes **in-** (meaning "in"), **in-** (meaning "not"), and **inter-**. If a student reads *A Voice from the Border* by Pamela Smith Hill (HarperTrophy, 2000), she might add the following words to the Scavenger Hunt chart:

independent

intend

~~intensity~~

Use two different colors of markers or highlighters to identify the prefix and root of each word on the chart. Cross off any word students agree does not begin with an **in-** or **inter-** prefix.

Scavenger Hunt Homework

See page 44 for complete Scavenger Hunt Homework directions. Have students find one or more words that fit this month's hunt. Here is an example using *Molly McGinty Has a Really Good Day* by Gary Paulsen (Yearling, 2006).

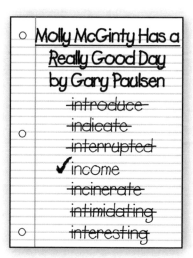

Molly McGinty Has a Really Good Day by Gary Paulsen
~~introduce~~
~~indicate~~
~~interrupted~~
✓income
~~incinerate~~
~~intimidating~~
~~interesting~~

Making Words

See page 25 for complete Making Words directions.

subfreezing

Letters: e e i u b f g n r s z

Make Words: use/sue, surf, rise, risen, using/suing, seize, reuse, refuse, seizure, surfing, reusing, refusing, freezing, subfreezing

Directions:

- Tell students how many letters to use to make each word.

- Emphasize how changing just one letter or rearranging letters makes a different word.

  "Add a letter to **reusing** to spell **refusing**."

  "Use the same letters in **using** to spell **suing**."

- When students are not just adding or changing one letter, cue them to start over.

  "Start over and use eight letters to spell **freezing**."

- Give meaning or sentence clues when needed to clarify the word they are making.

  "Start over and use five letters to spell **seize**. 'The Coast Guard was ordered to **seize** the ship and search it for stowaways.'"

- Give students one minute to figure out the secret word, then give clues if needed.

  "Our secret word is related to the word **freezing**."

Sort: Sort related words and use sentence clues to show how they are related.

seize, seizure

"When you **seize** something, you grab it or take it by force. This is called a **seizure**."

freezing, subfreezing

"When temperatures fall below the **freezing** level, we say they are **subfreezing**."

use, using, reuse, reusing

"When you **reuse** something, you **use** it again. The **e** is dropped before -**ing** is added to make **using** and **reusing**."

sue, suing, refuse, refusing

"The **e** is dropped before -**ing** is added to **sue** and **refuse** to make **suing** and **refusing**."

rise, risen

"We wait for the dough to **rise** and bake it once it has **risen**."

Reading Transfer: substandard, procedure

Tell students, "Pretend you are reading and come to a new word." Have students put the words under the appropriate related words and use the related words to decode them.

Spelling Transfer: failure, pressure

Tell students, "Pretend you are writing and need to spell each of these words." Have students tell you how each word begins. Then, have students find and use the appropriate related words to finish spelling each new word.

Making Words Homework
See page 28 for complete Making Words Homework directions. See page 153 for a Making Words Homework reproducible. Send the letters for **subfreezing** home with students to make and remake words.

Word Detectives

See page 28 for complete Word Detectives directions.

If the selected content word is **classification**, students might say the following words look like and sound like **classification**:

(classify)	vacation	donation
multiplication	(classified)	declaration
location	classroom	classic
station	imagination	expectation
reservation	nation	
evaporation	(class)	

Underline the parts that look similar and circle the related words. Remind students that related words often help in determining the meaning of the chosen content word.

Word Detectives Homework

See page 30 for complete Word Detectives Homework directions. Type the words students generate in the Word Detectives lesson or use the reproducibles on pages 154 or 155 to record them.

Option 1: Have students sort the words, add category headings, and add any additional words they know.

Option 2: Have students write the root word for each word on the list that has a root word.

Goal Two: Word Wall Words

Continue to gather students' writing samples to determine which words will be introduced and placed on the Word Wall.

- Be sure to highlight what makes the words illogical or difficult to spell.

- Students need to chant and write each word as it is introduced, then check each word by chanting their spellings as they touch each letter.

- Post the new words on the Word Wall. Hold students accountable for spelling the posted words correctly in all of their writing.

Word Wall Review Activities

Review Word Wall words throughout the week and month using the following activities.

Word Wall Riddles

See page 23 for complete directions for reviewing words using riddles.

Riddles focus students on particular features of each word in a game-like activity. For example, if you have placed the word **accept** on your Word Wall, your riddle might be, "Write the word that completes the sentence, 'Please _____ this gift as a token of my appreciation.'"

Word Wall Be a Mind Reader

See page 47 for complete Be a Mind Reader directions.

Select a word from the Word Wall. Give students five clues so that they can guess the word. For example, if you have added the word **people** to your Word Wall, you might use the following Be a Mind Reader lesson:

1. It is a word on the Word Wall.
2. It has two syllables.
3. It has three vowels.
4. It has two **e**'s.
5. The word means "more than one person."

Goal Three: Visual Checking System

What Looks Right?

See page 33 for complete What Looks Right? directions.

air	care	wear
awair	aware	awear
unfair	unfare	unfear
repair	repare	repear
midair	midare	midear
impair	impare	impear
compair	compare	compear
prepair	prepare	prepear
fanfair	fanfare	fanfear
airfair	airfare	airfear
debonair	debonare	debonear
welfair	welfare	welfear
sportswair	sportsware	sportswear
wheelchair	wheelchare	wheelchear
formalwair	formalware	formalwear

Goal Four: Cross-Checking

Guess the Covered Word

See page 34 for complete Guess the Covered Word directions. Here is a possible Guess the Covered Word lesson adapted from a Web site developed by Gordon Russell Middle School in Gresham, Oregon:

Molly Pitcher

A woman named Mary married a **soldier** named John Casper Hays. When he enlisted in the Colonial artillery in 1775, Mary **followed** John all the way into the battlefield. During the cruel Battle of Monmouth, Mary would bring pitchers of water from a nearby **creek** to the thirsty soldiers. This act of **courage** and kindness earned Mary the nickname "Molly Pitcher." Molly's acts did not stop at the **pitcher**. When Molly's husband collapsed while manning his **cannon**, Molly took over for him. This brought attention to Molly from George Washington, who **complimented** her works.

April

Month at a Glance

There are no more Nifty Thrifty Fifty words, so Word Wall words can be introduced at the beginning of the month. This gives you more time to review all of the words. Look for the transfer of what has been learned in Working with Words to students' reading and writing. This will help you decide which words need the most review work. The end of the year is just around the corner! Make the most of every opportunity you have to teach words.

Here are the major things you will do during Working with Words in April to help students move toward meeting all four goals:

- **Goal One:** Polysyllabic Words

  All of the Nifty Thrifty Fifty words are on the Word Wall. Use extra time to review the words with Be a Mind Reader, Riddles, and Mini-WORDO. Use the suggested Word Sort to extend understanding of the prefix **inter-** and the root words **nation** and **sign**. Use the Scavenger Hunt to review **anti-** words. Have students use the Nifty Thrifty Fifty Cards to explore combinations of prefixes, suffixes, and root words for all 50 words. Use the Making Words lesson to work with the suffix **-ation**, the prefix **re-**, and the root word **sign**. Use the Word Detectives lesson to help students use the prefixes and suffixes of content-area words to determine meanings.

- **Goal Two:** Word Wall Words

  Choose 8–10 more words from students' writing and add these to the Word Wall. Use spare minutes to review and practice all of the words through chanting and writing, Word Wall Riddles, and Be a Mind Reader activities. Hold students accountable for these words in all of their writing.

- **Goal Three:** Visual Checking System

  Use the What Looks Right? lesson to focus on the **ue**, **ew**, and **oo** patterns.

- **Goal Four:** Cross-Checking

  Use Guess the Covered Word lessons to introduce content-area vocabulary or highlight a part of speech. This month, you might consider choosing excerpts from science texts.

Goal One: Polysyllabic Words

Nifty Thrifty Fifty Review Activities

Nifty Thrifty Fifty Be a Mind Reader

See page 47 for complete Be a Mind Reader directions.

1. It is a Nifty Thrifty Fifty word.
2. It has a prefix that means "opposite."
3. It has nine letters.
4. It begins with a **d**. (discovery, dishonest, deodorize)
5. It has three syllables. (dishonest)

1. It is a Nifty Thrifty Fifty word.
2. It has eight letters.
3. It has a prefix or a suffix but not both.
4. It has three vowels. (forecast, prettier)
5. It has two syllables. (forecast)

1. It is a Nifty Thrifty Fifty word.
2. It has a spelling change.
3. It has a prefix and a suffix.
4. It begins with the letter **i**. (invasion, irresponsible)
5. It fits in the sentence, "Coming into the bathroom was an _____ of my privacy." (invasion)

1. It is a Nifty Thrifty Fifty word.
2. It has three syllables.
3. It is a noun.
4. It does not have a spelling change. (governor, musician, performance, submarine)
5. It is the longest word with no spelling changes. (performance)

1. It is a Nifty Thrifty Fifty word.
2. It has a suffix but no prefix.
3. It has three syllables.
4. It does not have a spelling change. (classify, different, governor, musician, signature)
5. It fits in the sentence, "You must write your _____ on the back of the check to cash it." (signature)

1. It is a Nifty Thrifty Fifty word.
2. It has nine letters.
3. It has a prefix and a suffix.
4. It does not have a spelling change. (deodorize, discovery)
5. It is what you do to make something smell nice. (deodorize)

1. It is a Nifty Thrifty Fifty word.
2. It has a prefix and a suffix.
3. It has four syllables.
4. It has at least 11 letters. (prehistoric, supermarkets)
5. It fits in the sentence, "I can find many different kinds of vegetables in _____." (supermarkets)

1. It is a Nifty Thrifty Fifty word.
2. It has four syllables.
3. It is the only word listed under its beginning letter.
4. It has at least four vowels. (overpower, transportation)
5. It fits in the sentence, "He tried to _____ the guard and escape." (overpower)

Nifty Thrifty Fifty Riddles

See page 23 for complete directions for using riddles to review words.

Have each student number a piece of paper to correspond with the number of words you have time to review. Give the following clues for the Nifty Thrifty Fifty words introduced this year.

1. This word means "to give courage to someone." (encouragement)
2. Write the word that is an antonym for **cheap**. (expensive)
3. Write the word that is a synonym for **neighborhoods**. (communities)
4. This word means the same as **disagreeable**. (unpleasant)
5. This word is an antonym for **trustworthy**. (irresponsible)
6. This word is a synonym for **misinterpret**. (misunderstand)
7. Write the word that means the same as **global**. (international)

Have each student check her own paper by chanting the letters in each word aloud again and underlining each letter as she says it.

Nifty Thrifty Fifty Mini-WORDO

See page 37 for complete Mini-WORDO directions.

Have students write the following Nifty Thrifty Fifty words on their blank Mini-WORDO cards.

deodorize	antifreeze	beautiful
classify	overpower	expensive
communities	forecast	composer

Possible combined words to show and say:

forecaster	freezer	overcast
powerful	expenses	declassify

Beyond Nifty Thrifty Fifty
Nifty Thrifty Fifty Cards

See page 24 for directions for using Nifty Thrifty Fifty Cards to make new words.

Words to make: prearranged, misplacement

Ask students to make their own words from the morphemes.

Neologism to make: interarrangeable

Ask a student to use the neologism in a sensible sentence. Be sure the sentence defines the word as "things that can be arranged between two or more places." For example, "Food on the dinner table is interarrangeable."

Ask students to make their own neologisms. Suggest that they make up riddles or say sentences that will help other students discover the spelling and meaning of their neologisms.

Nifty Thrifty Fifty Cards Homework

See page 25 for complete Nifty Thrifty Fifty Cards Homework directions. Have each student take home the March Morpheme chart (pages 139–140) to make two additional words and one additional neologism. Have students write riddles or defining sentences for their neologisms.

Word Sorts

See page 39 for complete Prefix and Suffix Sorts directions.

Prefix Sort: inter-

(from the Nifty Thrifty Fifty word **international**, introduced in February)

inter- (prefix) among; between; within	spelling/pronunciation only

See page 148 for a reproducible of this prefix sort. To introduce this sort you might say, "**International** is the root word **nation** with the prefix **inter-** and the suffix -**al**. **Inter-** often means 'between.' **International** fits in the first column. **Interest** begins with **i-n-t-e-r** but **est** isn't a root word, so **interest** fits in the second column."

Show and say the following words one at a time and have students put each word in the correct column:

interaction   interfere   intercontinental   intern   internalize   intermediate

interoffice   interpret   interstate   interrupt   interview

inter- (prefix) among; between; within	spelling/pronunciation only
international	interest
interaction	interfere
intercontinental	intern
intermediate	internalize
interoffice	interpret
interstate	interrupt
interview	

Root Word Lessons
See page 42 for complete Root Word Lessons directions.

Root Word Lesson: nation
(from Nifty Thrifty Fifty word **international**, introduced in February)

Definition: people in one land under a single government; a community of people or peoples who live in a defined territory and are organized under a single government

Write these words:

nation   nationalize

Students might suggest:

national   nationalism   nationality   nations   international

Root Word Lesson: sign
(from the Nifty Thrifty Fifty word **signature**, introduced in February)

Definition: something representing something else; an advertising notice; a symbol used in math or logic; a musical notation symbol

Write these words:

sign   signpost

Students might suggest:

design   resign   signed   designer   signaled

Scavenger Hunt

See page 42 for complete Scavenger Hunt directions.

The suggested hunt for April is for words with the **anti-** prefix. If a student reads *World War II for Kids: A History with 21 Activities* by Richard Panchyk (Chicago Review Press, 2002), he might add the following words with the **anti-** prefix to the Scavenger Hunt chart:

anti-Semitism

antiaircraft

antitank

Use two different colors of markers or highlighters to identify the prefix and root of each word on the chart. Cross off any word students agree does not have the **anti-** prefix.

Scavenger Hunt Homework

See page 44 for complete Scavenger Hunt Homework directions. Have each student find one or more words that fit this month's hunt. Here is an example using *A Three-Minute Speech: Lincoln's Remarks at Gettysburg* by Jennifer Armstrong (Aladdin, 2003).

A
Three-Minute Speech:
Lincoln's Remarks at
Gettysburg
by
Jennifer Armstrong
✓ antislavery

Making Words

See page 25 for complete Making Words directions.

resignation

Letters: a e i i o g n n r s t

Make Words: rain, sing/sign, sting, singer/signer/resign, ignore, origin, stinger, ignorant, rainiest, originate, resignation

Directions:

- Tell students how many letters to use to make each word.

- Emphasize how changing just one letter or rearranging letters makes a different word.

  "Use the same letters in **singer** to spell **signer**. Use those letters again to spell **resign**."

- When students are not just adding or changing one letter, cue them to start over.

  "Start over and use eight letters to spell **rainiest**."

- Give meaning or sentence clues when needed to clarify the word students are making.

    "Start over and use six letters to spell **origin**. 'The coach questioned all of the team members to find the **origin** of the rumor.'"

- Give students one minute to figure out the secret word, and then give clues if needed.

    "Our secret word is related to the words **sign** and **resign**."

Sort: Sort related words and use sentence clues to show how they are related.

rain, rainiest

"We got 10 inches of **rain** in June, making it the **rainiest** June on record."

sing, singer

"If you **sing**, you are a **singer**."

sting, stinger

"A bee can **sting** you with its **stinger**."

ignore, ignorant

"When you don't notice something, you **ignore** it. A person who is **ignorant** does not pay attention to what is happening around him."

origin, originate

"An **origin** is where something comes from. Humans **originate** from Earth."

sign, signer, resign, resignation

"If you **sign** something, you are a **signer**. When you **resign**, you quit and "sign back" your job. This is called a **resignation**."

Reading Transfer: design, designation

Tell students, "Pretend you are reading and come to a new word." Have students put the words under the appropriate related words and use the related words to decode them.

Spelling Transfer: pleasant, resistant

Tell students, "Pretend you are writing and need to spell each of these words." Have students tell you how each word begins. Then, have students find and use the appropriate related words to finish spelling each new word.

Making Words Homework

See page 28 for complete Making Words Homework directions. See page 153 for a Making Words Homework reproducible. Send the letters for **resignation** home with students to make and remake words.

Word Detectives

See page 28 for complete Word Detectives directions.

If the selected content-area word is **desegregation**, students might say the following words look like and sound like **desegregation**:

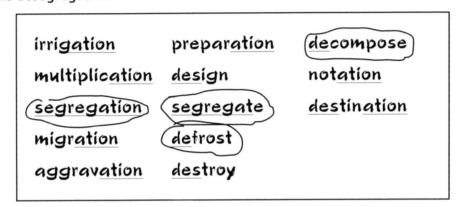

Underline the parts that look similar and circle the related words. Remind students that related words often help with determining the meaning of the chosen content word.

Word Detectives Homework

See page 30 for complete Word Detectives Homework directions. Type the words students generate in the Word Detectives lesson or use the reproducibles on pages 154 or 155 to record them.

Option 1: Have students sort the words, add category headings, and add any additional words they know.

Option 2: Have students write the root word for each word on the list that has a root word.

Goal Two: Word Wall Words

Continue to gather students' writing samples to determine which words will be introduced and placed on the wall.

- Be sure to highlight what makes the words illogical or difficult to spell.

- Students need to chant and write each word as it is introduced, then check each word by chanting their spellings as they touch each letter.

- Post the new words on the Word Wall. Hold students accountable for spelling the posted words correctly in all of their writing.

Word Wall Review Activities

Review Word Wall words throughout the week and month using the following activities.

Word Wall Riddles

See page 23 for complete directions for reviewing words using riddles.

Riddles focus students' attention on particular features of each word in a game-like activity. For example, if you have placed the word **was** on your Word Wall, your riddle might be, "Write the word that completes the sentence, 'I wanted to play outside yesterday, but it ____ raining.'"

Word Wall Be a Mind Reader

See page 47 for complete Be a Mind Reader directions.

Select a word from the Word Wall. Give students five clues so that they can guess the word. For example, if you have added the word **were** to your Word Wall, you might use the following Be a Mind Reader lesson:

1. It is a word on the Word Wall.
2. It has one syllable.
3. It is a four-letter word.
4. It has two **e**'s.
5. It begins with a **w**.

Goal Three: Visual Checking System

What Looks Right?

See page 33 for complete What Looks Right? directions.

true	new	zoo
renue	renew	renoo
kazue	kazew	kazoo
avenue	avenew	avenoo
curfue	curfew	curfoo
miscue	miscew	miscoo
pursue	pursew	persoo
bambue	bambew	bamboo
outgrue	outgrew	outgroo
revenue	revenew	revenoo
kangarue	kangarew	kangaroo
corkscrue	corkscrew	corkscroo
misconstrue	misconstrew	misconstroo

Goal Four: Cross-Checking

Guess the Covered Word

See page 34 for complete Guess the Covered Word directions. Here is a possible Guess the Covered Word lesson adapted from *Lightning* by Seymour Simon (HarperTrophy, 1999):

Lightning

Lightning bolts **travel** at a "lightning" speed of up to 60,000 miles per second. That's 6,000 times faster than our fastest **spaceships**. A single lightning bolt travels through twisted paths in the air about as wide as one of your **fingers** and from 6 to 10 miles long.

Lightning **begins** with violently moving ice crystals and raindrops in storm clouds. As a result of the **motion**, electric charges build up at the bottom of the cloud. An opposite electric charge builds up in the **ground** just below the cloud. The charges in the ground can make your hair stand on end right before a lightning **storm**.

May/June

Month at a Glance

It is the last two months of school, and your students have been busy learning about big words. They have also been working with Word Wall words to improve the frequently used, frequently misspelled words that haunt their writing. Again, be sure to introduce your last group of Word Wall words at the beginning of the month so that you will have the full month to work with them. Continue reviewing the Nifty Thrifty Fifty, and encourage students to be on the lookout in their summer reading for words that are related!

Here are the major things you will do during Working with Words in May/June to help students move toward meeting all four goals:

- **Goal One:** Polysyllabic Words

  All of the Nifty Thrifty Fifty words are on the Word Wall. Use extra time to review the words with Be a Mind Reader, Riddles, and Mini-WORDO. Use the suggested Word Sort to extend the understanding of the prefixes **pre-**, **il-**, **ir-**, **im-**, and **in-**, and the root word **market**. Use the Scavenger Hunt to review -**tion**/-**ation** words. Have students use the Nifty Thrifty Fifty Cards to explore combinations of prefixes, suffixes, and root words for all 50 words. Use the Making Words lesson to work with the suffixes -**ic**, -**al**, and -**ly**, and the root word **history**. Use the Word Detectives lesson to help students use the prefixes and suffixes of content-area words to determine meanings.

- **Goal Two:** Word Wall Words

  Choose 8–10 more words from students' writing and add these to the Word Wall. Use spare minutes to review and practice all of the words through chanting and writing, Word Wall Riddles, and Be a Mind Reader activities. Hold students accountable for these words in all of their writing.

- **Goal Three:** Visual Checking System

  Use the What Looks Right? lesson to focus on the **le**, **el**, and **al** patterns.

- **Goal Four:** Cross-Checking

  Use Guess the Covered Word lessons to introduce content-area vocabulary or highlight a part of speech. This month, you might consider adapting a movie review.

Goal One: Polysyllabic Words

Nifty Thrifty Fifty Review Activities
Nifty Thrifty Fifty Be a Mind Reader
See page 47 for complete Be a Mind Reader directions.

1. It is a Nifty Thrifty Fifty word.
2. It has five vowels.
3. It has a prefix and a suffix.
4. It has more than 10 letters. (independence, irresponsible)
5. It describes someone who doesn't take care of things. (irresponsible)

1. It is a Nifty Thrifty Fifty word.
2. It has three syllables.
3. It has three vowels; two are the same letter.
4. It has nine letters. (different, forgotten, nonliving)
5. It has a suffix with no spelling change and no prefix. (different)

1. It is a Nifty Thrifty Fifty word.
2. It has a prefix and a suffix.
3. It has eight letters.
4. It has three syllables. (composer, employee, invasion)
5. There are no spelling changes. (employee)

1. It is a Nifty Thrifty Fifty word.
2. It has a suffix but no prefix.
3. It has a spelling change.
4. It has three syllables. (beautiful, forgotten, happiness, nonliving)
5. It fits in the sentence, "Money doesn't buy _____." (happiness)

1. It is a Nifty Thrifty Fifty word.
2. It has a prefix and a suffix.
3. It has 13 letters.
4. It has five syllables. (international, irresponsible)
5. It has no spelling changes. (international)

1. It is a Nifty Thrifty Fifty word.
2. It has a prefix but no suffix.
3. It has eight letters.
4. It has two syllables. (forecast, midnight)
5. It fits in the sentence, "The old year ended at _____." (midnight)

1. It is a Nifty Thrifty Fifty word.
2. It has four syllables.
3. It has four vowels.
4. It has a prefix and a suffix. (prehistoric, supermarkets)
5. It refers to something that is very old. (prehistoric)

Nifty Thrifty Fifty Riddles

See page 23 for complete directions for reviewing words using riddles.

Have each student number a piece of paper to correspond to the number of words you have time to review.

Here are some suggested clues for the Nifty Thrifty Fifty words introduced this year:

1. Write the word that is an antonym for **achievable**. (impossible)

2. This word is a synonym for **grocery stores**. (supermarkets)

3. Write the word that is an antonym for **unattractive**. (beautiful)

4. This word means the same as **uninterrupted**. (continuous)

5. This word is a synonym for **recital**. (performance)

6. Write the word that means the same as **substitution**. (replacement)

7. Write the word that means the same as **diverse**. (different)

Have each student check her own paper by chanting the letters in each word aloud again and underlining each letter as she says it.

Nifty Thrifty Fifty Mini-WORDO

See page 37 for complete Mini-WORDO directions.

Have students write the following Nifty Thrifty Fifty words on their blank Mini-WORDO cards.

midnight	impression	dishonest
unfriendly	composer	encouragement
supermarkets	happiness	swimming

Possible combined words to show and say:

marketing	nightly	discouraging	superimpose
compression	friendliness	unhappy	

Beyond Nifty Thrifty Fifty
Nifty Thrifty Fifty Cards
See page 24 for complete directions for using Nifty Thrifty Fifty Cards to make new words.

Words to make: nationalization, empowering

Ask students to make their own words from the morphemes.

Neologism to make: antihistoration

Ask a student to use the word in a sensible sentence. Be sure the sentence defines the word as, "against the action or process of recording history." For example, "A government that is embarrassed by something it did would be in favor of antihistoration."

Ask students to make their own neologisms. Suggest that they make up riddles or say sentences that will help other students discover the spelling and meaning of their neologisms.

Nifty Thrifty Fifty Cards Homework

See page 25 for complete Nifty Thrifty Fifty Cards Homework directions. Have each student take home the March Morpheme chart (pages 139–140) to make two additional words and one additional neologism. Have students write riddles or defining sentences for their neologisms.

Word Sorts

See page 39 for complete Prefix and Suffix Sorts directions.

Prefix Sort: pre-

(from the Nifty Thrifty Fifty word **prehistoric**, introduced in February)

pre- (prefix) before	spelling/pronunciation only	part of the word/ different pronunciation

See page 148 for a reproducible of this prefix sort. To introduce this sort you might say, "**Prehistoric** is the root word **history** with the prefix **pre-** and the suffix **-ic**. The prefix **pre-** means 'before.' **Prehistoric** fits in the first column. **Prefer** begins with **p-r-e** but **fer** isn't a root word, so **prefer** fits in the second column. **Pretty** also starts with **p-r-e** but **tty** isn't a word. The **p-r-e** in **pretty** doesn't sound like the **p-r-e** in prehistoric, so **pretty** belongs in the last column."

Show and say the following words one at a time and have students put each word in the correct column:

present	preheat	pretend	preserve	preview	preschool

prepare	premature	president	pressure	premium	preteen

pre- (prefix) before	spelling/pronunciation only	part of the word/ different pronunciation
prehistoric	prefer	pretty
preheat	pretend	present
preview	preserve	president
preschool	prepare	pressure
premature	premium	
preteen		

Prefix Combination Sort: il-, ir-, im-, in-

(**il-** from the Nifty Thrifty Fifty word **illegal**, introduced in January; **ir-** from the Nifty Thrifty Fifty word **irresponsible**, introduced in January; **im-** from the Nifty Thrifty Fifty word **impossible**, introduced in August/September; **in-** from the Nifty Thrifty Fifty word **independence**, introduced in October)

il-, ir-, im-, in- (prefixes) opposite	spelling/pronunciation only

See page 149 for a reproducible of this prefix combination sort. To introduce this sort you might say, "All of these words begin with prefixes that change the root word to an opposite meaning. **Illegal** is the word **legal** with the prefix **il-**. **Illegal** means 'not legal,' so **illegal** goes in the first column. **Irresponsible** is the word **response** with the prefix **ir-** and the suffix -**ible**. If you are **irresponsible**, then you are unable to take responsibility, so **irresponsible** also belongs in the first column. **Impossible** is the root word **possible** with the prefix **im-**. **Impossible** is the opposite of **possible**, so **impossible** fits in the first column. **Independence** is the root word **depend** with the prefix **in-** and the suffix -**ence**. **Independence** is the opposite of **dependence**, so it also belongs in the first column. **Insulate** begins with **i-n**, but **sulate** isn't a root word, so **insulate** fits in the second column."

Show and say the following words one at a time and have students put each word in the correct column:

imperfection	inexpensive	illustrate	illiteracy	instant	inescapable	irrigate
instrument	irregular	imagine	insincere	irresistible	inactive	impure
illustrator	implying	imperfect	irritate	irreversible	improve	inability
incomplete	impolite	illustration	instance	inaccurate	imitator	

il-, ir-, im-, in- (prefixes) opposite	spelling/pronunciation only
illegal	insulate
irresponsible	illustrate
impossible	instant
independence	irrigate
imperfection	instrument
inexpensive	imagine
illiteracy	illustrator
inescapable	implying
irregular	irritate
insincere	imitator
irresistible	illustration
imperfect	improve
inactive	instance
irreversible	
impure	
impolite	
inability	
inaccurate	
incomplete	

Root Word Lessons

See page 42 for complete Root Word Lessons directions.

Root Word Lesson: market

(from the Nifty Thrifty Fifty word **supermarkets**, introduced in March)

Definition: a gathering for buying or selling; a gathering of people who sell things, especially food or animals, in a place open to the public or other buyers

Write these words:

supermarkets   submarket

Students might suggest:

supermarket   marketer   marketing   marketed   marketplace

Scavenger Hunt

See page 42 for complete Scavenger Hunt directions.

The suggested hunt for May/June is for words that end with the suffix -**tion**/-**ation**. If a student reads *Punctuation Takes a Vacation* by Robin Pulver (Holiday House, 2004), he might add the following words to the Scavenger Hunt chart:

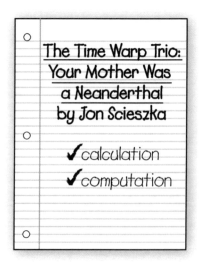

drop e **punctuation**	drop d **attention**
drop e **vacation**	drop e **quotation**
~~question~~	drop e **abbreviation**

Use two different colors of markers to identify the root and suffix of each word on the chart. If there is a spelling change, write what changed above the root. Cross off any word students agree does not end with the suffix -**tion**/-**ation**.

Scavenger Hunt Homework

See page 44 for complete Scavenger Hunt Homework directions. Have each student find two or more words that fit this month's hunt. Here is an example using *The Time Warp Trio: Your Mother Was a Neanderthal* by Jon Scieszka (Puffin, 2004).

The Time Warp Trio:
Your Mother Was
a Neanderthal
by Jon Scieszka

✔ calculation
✔ computation

Making Words

See page 25 for complete Making Words directions.

historically

Letters: a i i o c h l l r s t y

Make Words: rich, hill, chill, hilly, hasty, short, chilly, social, richly, shortly, hastily, history, socially, historic, historically

Directions:

- Tell students how many letters to use to make each word.

- Emphasize how changing just one letter or rearranging letters makes a different word.

  "Add a letter to **hill** to spell **chill**."

- When students are not just adding or changing one letter, cue them to start over.

  "Start over and use eight new letters to spell **historic**."

- Give meaning or sentence clues when needed to clarify the word they are making.

  "Start over and use five new letters to spell **hasty**. 'Grandma wanted to sell her house, but Mom asked her not to make any **hasty** decisions.'"

- Give students one minute to figure out the secret word, then give clues if needed.

  "Our secret word is related to the word **history**."

Sort: Sort related words and use sentence clues to show how they are related.

history, historic, historically

"We lived in an old house in the **historic** district. The house was 200 years old and was there through most of our town's **history**. I wrote a report about the house and used the library to make sure my information was **historically** accurate."

hill, hilly

"After we climbed the fourth **hill**, my father said, 'This area is **hilly**.'"

chill, chilly

"When the air has a **chill** in it, it is **chilly**."

short, shortly

"If you are going to do something in a **short** while, you say, 'I will do it **shortly**.'"

hasty, hastily

"He was **hasty** when he worked, so he worked **hastily**."

rich, richly

"The poor man who was **rich** in his heart was **richly** rewarded for his bravery and courage."

social, socially

"A society is a group that shares certain traditions and expectations. If something is not **socially** acceptable, it is not acceptable to the people in a certain **social** group."

Reading Transfer: magically, practically

Tell students, "Pretend you are reading and come to a new word." Have students put the words under the appropriate related words and use the related words to decode them.

Spelling Transfer: quickly, sleepy

Tell students, "Pretend you are writing and need to spell each of these words." Have students tell you how each word begins. Then, have students find and use the appropriate related words to finish spelling each new word.

Making Words Homework

See page 28 for complete Making Words Homework directions. See page 153 for a Making Words Homework reproducible. Send the letters for **historically** home with students to make and remake words.

Word Detectives

See page 28 for complete Word Detectives directions. If the selected content-area word is **expression**, students might say the following words look like and sound like **expression**:

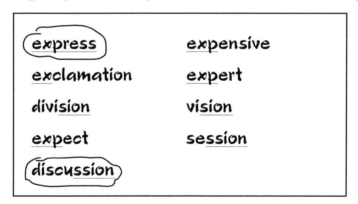

Underline the parts that look similar and circle the related words. Remind students that related words often help in determining the meaning of the chosen content word.

Word Detectives Homework

See page 30 for complete Word Detectives Homework directions. Type the words students generate in the Word Detectives lesson or use the reproducibles on pages 154 or 155 to record them.

Option 1: Have students sort the words, add category headings, and add any additional words they know.

Option 2: Have students write the root word for each word on the list that has a root word.

Goal Two: Word Wall Words

Continue to gather students' writing samples to determine which words will be introduced and placed on the Word Wall.

- Be sure to highlight what makes the words illogical or difficult to spell.

- Students need to chant and write each word as it is introduced, then check each word by chanting their spellings as they touch each letter.

- Post the new words on the Word Wall. Hold students accountable for spelling the posted words correctly in all of their writing.

Word Wall Review Activities

Review Word Wall words throughout the week and month using the following activities.

Word Wall Riddles

See page 23 for complete directions for reviewing words using riddles.

Riddles focus students on particular features of each word in a game-like activity. For example, if you have placed the word **could** on your Word Wall, your riddle might be, "Write the word that rhymes with **would**."

Word Wall Be a Mind Reader

See page 47 for complete Be a Mind Reader directions.

Select a word from the Word Wall. Give students five clues so that they can guess the word. For example, if you have added the word **thought** to your Word Wall, you might use the following Be a Mind Reader lesson:

1. It is a word on the Word Wall.
2. It has one syllable.
3. It begins with a **t**.
4. It has two vowels.
5. It has a **th** and a **gh**.

Goal Three: Visual Checking System

What Looks Right?

See page 33 for complete What Looks Right? directions.

people	model	animal
petle	petel	petal
gavle	gavel	gaval
pedle	pedel	pedal
medle	medel	medal
bottle	bottel	bottal
travle	travel	traval
peddle	peddel	peddal
funnle	funnel	funnal
coddle	coddel	coddal
kettle	kettel	kettal
unravle	unravel	unraval
Aristotle	Aristotel	Aristotal

Goal Four: Cross-Checking

Guess the Covered Word

See page 34 for complete Guess the Covered Word directions. Here is a possible Guess the Covered Word lesson that focuses on verbs. It is an excerpt from a *USAToday* movie review.

Parts of Speech: Verbs

The Shaggy Dog may not make you **howl**, but it does offer a few bona fide belly laughs, which is more than the last few Tim Allen movies could boast. Allen plays assistant district attorney Dave Douglas, who is **prosecuting** an animal-rights activist for a fire set at a mysterious medical lab. A genetically mutated dog escapes from the lab and is **taken** in by Douglas's family. Douglas, no fan of dogs, is bitten and gradually **transforms** into a part-time dog. **Morphing** into man's best friend teaches him a thing or two about being a good father.

Nifty Thrifty Fifty

Word	Prefix	Suffix		Word	Prefix	Suffix
antifreeze	anti-			international	inter-	-al
beautiful		-ful (y to i)		invasion*	in-	-sion
classify		-ify		irresponsible*	ir-	-ible
communities*	com-	-es (y to i)		midnight	mid-	
community*	com-			misunderstand	mis-	
composer*	com-	-er		musician		-ian
continuous*	con-	-ous		nonliving	non-	-ing (drop e)
conversation*	con-	-tion		overpower	over-	
deodorize	de-	-ize		performance*	per-	-ance
different		-ent		prehistoric	pre-	-ic
discovery	dis-	-y		prettier		-er (y to i)
dishonest	dis-			rearrange	re-	
electricity		-ity		replacement	re-	-ment
employee*	em-	-ee		richest		-est
encouragement	en-	-ment		semifinal	semi-	
expensive*	ex-	-ive		signature		-ture
forecast	fore-			submarine	sub-	
forgotten		-en (double t)		supermarkets	super-	-s
governor		-or		swimming		-ing (double m)
happiness		-ness (y to i)		transportation	trans-	-tion
hopeless		-less		underweight	under-	
illegal*	il-			unfinished	un-	-ed
impossible*	im-			unfriendly	un-	-ly
impression*	im-	-ion		unpleasant	un-	-ant (drop e)
independence*	in-	-ence		valuable		-able (drop e)

* Indicates an unpeelable prefix.

Priority Word Lists

Words to Choose from for Upper Grade Word Wall

First Priority: High-Frequency, Commonly Misspelled Words

again
There are many words with first syllables that begin with **a** and are pronounced like **again** (**about**, **above**, **ago**). The last syllable of **again** is spelled like **rain** and **train**. **Again** used to rhyme with **train** and **rain**, but the pronunciation has changed over time.

are
Other words that end in **are** rhyme with **care** and **spare**.

always
This is a word in which the first syllable could logically be spelled **a-l-l**.

because
Because sounds like it should be spelled **b-e-c-u-z** but is actually logical when you point out the word **cause** and the relationship between **cause** and **because**.

believe
Believe sounds like it should be spelled **b-e-l-e-a-v-e**.

could
There is no explanation for the spelling of **could**. Students may take some consolation in the fact that when they have learned **could**, they can use the same illogical pattern to spell **should** and **would**.

during
During seems like it should be spelled with a double **r** like in **purring** and **stirring**.

enough
Again, there is no explanation for the spelling of the last syllable of **enough**, but once students can spell it they can also spell **rough** and **tough**.

friends
What is the **i** doing there? It may help students if you point out that friends "ends" with **e-n-d-s**.

favorite
The word **favor** is spelled correctly. Many words that end like **favorite** (**definite**, **opposite**, **granite**) are spelled **i-t-e**.

laugh
There is no reason for **laugh** to be spelled in this funny "laughable" way.

people

This is the only word in which **e-o** spells the **e** sound.

perhaps

This word can be confusing because some may think it ends with a double **p**, because of words like **happiness** and **sappy**.

said

Said should rhyme with **paid** and **braid**, and it used to. The pronunciation changed but the spelling did not.

they

There is no reason **they** should not be spelled **t-h-a-y**, but it isn't!

then

Then is spelled logically but often misspelled as **t-h-i-n** or **t-h-a-n**, particularly if pronounced like those words.

terrible

This is a logical word but is often misspelled with only one **r** or with an **e-l** at the end.

thought

This is an illogical spelling, but the same pattern is used in other words including **ought**, **bought**, and **brought**.

trouble

Here is another illogical spelling, but the same pattern is used in the word **double**.

until

Students may ask, "Where is the double **l** that ends all other rhyming words?"

very

Most words rhyming with **very** have two **r**'s (**berry**, **merry**, etc.), but **very** is spelled just like the **every** students have been spelling in **everyone**, **everybody**, and **everything**.

want

Many **w-a** words have a funny pronunciation and follow their own strange **w-a** patterns: **was**, **wad**, **wash**, **war**, **watch**, **warm**, **warp**, etc.

was

This is one of those **w-a** words like **want**. The **s** at the end of this word sounds like **z**, as in other words, such as **is**, **has**, and **does**.

went

This word is not illogical but is often misspelled **w-i-n-t**, especially if pronounced like that.

Priority Word Lists ···

when
This word is not illogical but is often misspelled **w**-**i**-**n**, especially if pronounced like that.

what
Other words spelled like this rhyme with **at**, **cat**, and **that**.

who
This is a totally illogical spelling for this word.

with
This is a logical word but is still often misspelled.

were
Were is another **w** word with an illogical spelling.

Second Priority: Common Contractions and Compounds

can't	wouldn't	yourself
don't	another	ourselves
didn't	anyone	sometimes
doesn't	everybody	themselves
let's	something	throughout
that's	cannot	upon
won't	however	

Not Compounds but Students Write Them as Compounds

a lot	all right	no one

Third Priority: Common Homophones

accept	it's	right	they're
except	knew	write	we're
by	new	threw	wear
buy	know	through	where
hole	no	to	weather
whole	one	too (too much!)	whether
hour	won	two (#2)	your
our	quiet	their	you're
its	quite	there	

Fourth Priority: Spelling Change Examples: (doubling, drop **e**, **y** to **i**)

getting	biggest	funnier
hidden	exciting	prettiest
winner	countries	happiness
stopped	tried	
swimming	beautiful	

Fifth Priority: Other Homophones

board	bear	flea	plain
bored	beat	flour	plane
close	beet	flower	road
clothes	berry	heal	rode
hear	bury	heel	sea
here	break	knot	see
heard	brake	not	son
herd	cell	knight	sun
piece	sell	night	stake
peace	cent	mail	steak
wait	sent	male	weak
weight	scent	sail	week
ate	dear	sale	wood
eight	deer	pail	would
bare	flee	pale	

Sixth Priority: Less Common Homophones; Other Commonly Misspelled Words

Less Common Homophones

desert	capital	council	gorilla
dessert	capitol	counsel	guerilla
aloud	compliment	genes	patience
allowed	complement	jeans	patients

Priority Word Lists ···

pole	wrap	suite	pare
poll	scene	sweet	pear
presence	seen	waist	soared
presents	soar	waste	sword
principal	sore	morning	
principle	stairs	mourning	
rap	stares	pair	

Other Commonly Misspelled Words

although	either	language	serious
America	embarrassed	machine	since
beneath	English	measure	soldiers
between	Europe	millions	special
bought	excellent	mountain	temperature
breathe	exercise	necessary	thousands
brought	experience	neighbor	together
caught	field	once	
century	foreign	particular	
certain	happened	president	
committee	height	receive	
country	important	recommend	
different	interesting	remember	
discussed	knowledge	restaurant	

Reproducibles

In the following section, you will find reproducibles for many of the lessons in this book. Below you will find directions for use of the reproducibles.

Page 133—Mini-WORDO Card

Make one copy of the blank Mini-WORDO card for each student. These cards will be used only one or two times, so plain paper is fine; card stock is not necessary. Students will write the nine Nifty Thrifty Fifty words you tell them on the card. They should write the words randomly on the card; their placement will determine who wins each round.

Pages 134–140—Morpheme Charts

There is a morpheme chart for each month of the school year. Each chart has a cumulative list of all of the morphemes students have learned so far with the Nifty Thrifty Fifty words. When you ask students to make two additional words by combining the word parts they have learned so far, this chart will be a helpful reference. The chart is also helpful when students make neologisms. It can be provided as a quick reference for students to have in their Big-Blocks Notebooks, as well.

Page 141–149—Word Sort Charts

These masters serve three purposes. When you are doing a class Word Sort, you can use the corresponding reproducible to make an overhead transparency for instruction and to make copies for the students to write on.

Page 150–152—Making Words Letter Strips

There is a Making Words letter strip for each monthly lesson. Make enough copies of each letter strip so that each student has his own strip. Then, have students cut the letters apart and write the capital letters on the back of each letter. Finally, have students use their individual letters to make the words in the lesson.

Page 153—Making Words Homework Sheet

Write the letters from the day's Making Words lesson in the boxes across the top of the page. Students should write as many words as they remember in the boxes below. In addition, they should write any new words they can come up with using the letters provided.

Page 154—Word Detectives Homework Sheet #1

Write the content word from the Word Detectives lesson in the box at the top of the sheet. In addition, write the words students brainstormed in the second box. Students should then rewrite the words in categories in the boxes below. If you decide to provide the categories, write those categories in the top row of boxes. Students will then write the words under the appropriate headings.

Reproducibles ···

Page 155—Word Detectives Homework Sheet #2

Write the content word from the Word Detectives lesson at the top of the sheet. In addition, write the words students brainstormed in the boxes on the left-hand side. Students should then write the corresponding root words in the boxes to the right of each word.

Page 156–157—Planning Sheets

These pages are aids for planning your instruction in the Working with Words block. You will find a sample sheet filled in on page 157 and a blank one for your use on page 156. The Planning Sheets help you organize three 20-minute lessons a week across four weeks (approximately a month) of instruction. The sheets also list the possible activities across the bottom as a reminder of your choices.

Page 158—Letter to Parents

This letter can be sent home with students to explain the lessons and activities they are doing during the Working with Words Block.

Recommended Professional Resources

Cunningham, P. M. (2005). *Big Words for Big Kids: Systematic Sequential Phonics and Spelling.* Greensboro, NC: Carson-Dellosa Publishing Company.

Cunningham, P. M. (2004). *Phonics They Use: Words for Reading and Writing* (4th edition). New York: Allyn & Bacon.

Cunningham, P. M. (1999). *Phonics They Use: Words for Reading and Writing* (3rd edition). New York: Allyn & Bacon.

Cunningham, P. M. and Hall, D. P. (1998). *Month-by-Month Phonics for Upper Grades: A Second Chance for Struggling Readers and Students Learning English.* Greensboro, NC: Carson-Dellosa Publishing Company.

Cunningham, P. M. and Hall, D. P. (1994). *Making Big Words: Multilevel, Hands-on Spelling and Phonics Activities.* Parsippany, NJ: Good Apple.

Cunningham, P. M. and Hall, D. P. (1997). *Making More Big Words.* Parsippany, NJ: Good Apple.

Young, S. (2006). *The Scholastic Rhyming Dictionary.* New York: Scholastic Reference.

Mini-WORDO

August/September Morpheme Chart

Prefix	Root	Suffix
com-	pose	-er
en-	courage	-ment
	hope	-less
dis-	cover	-y
un-	friend	-ly
	rich	-est
	music	-ian
im-	possible	

October Morpheme Chart

Prefix	Root	Suffix
com-	pose	-er
en-	courage	-ment
	hope	-less
dis-	cover	-y
un-	friend	-ly
	rich	-est
	music	-ian
im-	possible	
ex-	expense	-ive
	govern	-or
im-	press	-sion
in-	depend	-ence
sub-	marine	
trans-	port	-ation
un-	finish	-ed

Prefix	Root	Suffix
com-	pose	-er
en-	courage	-ment
	hope	-less
dis-	cover	-y
un-	friend	-ly
	rich	-est
	music	-ian
im-	possible	
ex-	expense	-ive
	govern	-or
im-	press	-sion
in-	depend	-ence
sub-	marine	
trans-	port	-ation
un-	finish	-ed
	beauty	-ful
	class	-ify
com-	unity	
com-	unity	-es
	electric	-ity
	happy	-ness
	pretty	-er

Prefix	Root	Suffix
com-	pose	-er
en-	courage	-ment
	hope	-less
dis-	cover	-y
un-	friend	-ly
	rich	-est
	music	-ian
im-	possible	
ex-	expense	-ive
	govern	-or
im-	press	-sion
in-	depend	-ence
sub-	marine	
trans-	port	-ation
un-	finish	-ed
	beauty	-ful
	class	-ify
com-	unity	
com-	unity	-es
	electric	-ity
	happy	-ness
	pretty	-er
con-	continue	-ous
non-	live	-ing
con-	converse	-ation
	swim	-ing
	value	-able
	forgot	-en
un-	please	-ant

Prefix	Root	Suffix
com-	pose	-er
en-	courage	-ment
	hope	-less
dis-	cover	-y
un-	friend	-ly
	rich	-est
	music	-ian
im-	possible	
ex-	expense	-ive
	govern	-or
im-	press	-sion
in-	depend	-ence
sub-	marine	
trans-	port	-ation
un-	finish	-ed
	beauty	-ful
	class	-ify
com-	unity	
com-	unity	-es
	electric	-ity
	happy	-ness
	pretty	-er
con-	continue	-ous
non-	live	-ing
con-	converse	-ation
	swim	-ing
	value	-able
	forgot	-en
un-	please	-ant
dis-	honest	
il-	legal	
ir-	response	-ible
mis-	understand	
per-	form	-ance
re-	arrange	
re-	place	-ment

Prefix	Root	Suffix
com-	pose	-er
en-	courage	-ment
	hope	-less
dis-	cover	-y
un-	friend	-ly
	rich	-est
	music	-ian
im-	possible	
ex-	expense	-ive
	govern	-or
im-	press	-sion
in-	depend	-ence
sub-	marine	
trans-	port	-ation
un-	finish	-ed
	beauty	-ful
	class	-ify
com-	unity	
com-	unity	-es
	electric	-ity
	happy	-ness
	pretty	-er
con-	continue	-ous
non-	live	-ing
con-	converse	-ation
	swim	-ing
	value	-able
	forgot	-en
un-	please	-ant
dis-	dishonest	
il-	legal	
ir-	response	-ible
mis-	understand	
per-	form	-ance
re-	arrange	
re-	place	-ment
de-	odor	-ize
	differ	-ent
em-	employ	-ee
inter-	nation	-al
in-	invade	-sion
pre-	history	-ic
	sign	-ature

Prefix	Root	Suffix
com-	pose	-er
en-	courage	-ment
	hope	-less
dis-	cover	-y
un-	friend	-ly
	rich	-est
	music	-ian
im-	possible	
ex-	expense	-ive
	govern	-or
im-	press	-sion
in-	depend	-ence
sub-	marine	
trans-	port	-ation
un-	finish	-ed
	beauty	-ful
	class	-ify
com-	unity	
com-	unity	-es
	electric	-ity
	happy	-ness
	pretty	-er
con-	continue	-ous
non-	live	-ing

(continued on page 140)

Prefix	Root	Suffix
con-	converse	-ation
	swim	-ing
	value	-able
	forgot	-en
un-	please	-ant
dis-	dishonest	
il-	legal	
ir-	response	-ible
mis-	understand	
per-	form	-ance
re-	arrange	
re-	place	-ment
de-	odor	-ize
	differ	-ent
em-	employ	-ee
inter-	nation	-al
in-	invade	-sion
pre-	history	-ic
	sign	-ature
anti-	freeze	
fore-	cast	
mid-	night	
semi-	final	
over-	power	
super-	market	-s
under-	weight	

October Prefix Sort: dis-

dis- (prefix) against, opposite, or apart	spelling/pronunciation only	part of the word/ different pronunciation
discovery	distinct	dishes

-ly (suffix)	spelling/pronunciation only	part of the word/ different pronunciation
unfriendly	folly	apply

im- (prefix) in	im- (prefix) opposite	spelling/pronunciation only
impression	impossible	image

December Suffix Sort: -en

-en (suffix) in	spelling/pronunciation only	part of the word/ different pronunciation
encouragement	enter	enough

- -

January Suffix Sort: -tion

-tion (suffix)	spelling/pronunciation only
conversation	nation

January Suffix Sort: -or

-or (suffix) someone or something that does	spelling/pronunciation only
governor	favor

February Suffix Sort: -ous

-ous (suffix) full of	spelling/pronunciation only
continuous	obnoxious

- -

February Prefix Sort: re-

re- (prefix) back or again	spelling/pronunciation only	part of the word/ different pronunciation
rearrange	resort	rectangular
replacement		

March Prefix Sort: ir-

ir- (prefix) opposite	spelling/pronunciation only	part of the word/ different pronunciation
irresponsible	irrigate	Iranian

- -

March Suffix Sort: -en

-en (suffix)	spelling/pronunciation only
forgotten	amen

April Prefix Sort: inter-

inter- (prefix) among; between; within	spelling/pronunciation only
international	interest

- - - - - - - - - - - - - - - - - - - -

May/June Prefix Sort: pre-

pre- (prefix) before	spelling/pronunciation only	part of the word/ different pronunciation
prehistoric	prefer	pretty

il-, ir-, im-, in- (prefixes) opposite	spelling/pronunciation only
illegal	insulate
irresponsible	
impossible	
independence	

encourage (August/September)

a e e e o u c g n r

independently (October)

e e e i d d l n n p t y

electrician (November)

a e e e i i c c l n r t

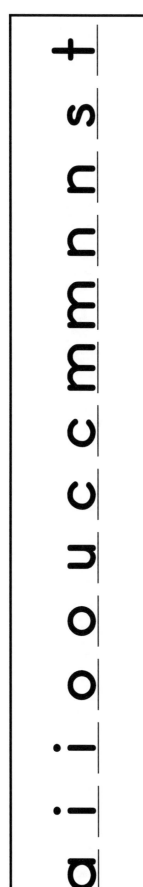

communications (December)

a i i o o u c c m m n n s t

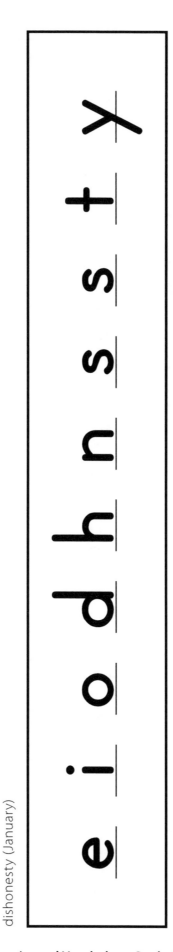

dishonesty (January)

e i o d h h n s s t y

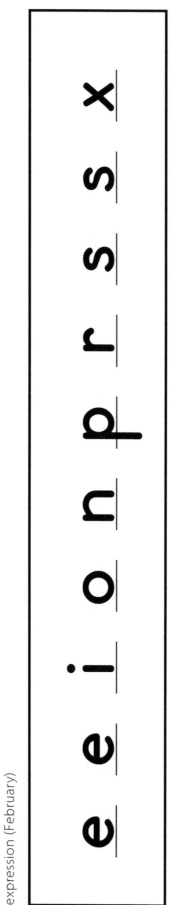

expression (February)

e e i o n p r s s x

subfreezing (March)

e e i u b f g n r s z

resignation (April)

a e i i o g n n r s t

historically (May/June)

a i i o c h l l r s t y

Making Words Homework Sheet

Word Detectives Homework Sheet #1

Content Word:

Words that look and sound like this word:

Write the words from the chart above in categories. Label your categories in the top row of boxes and add any new words to the categories that you can think of.

Word Detectives Homework Sheet #2

Content Word: _____

Words that look and sound like this word:

The words on the left are the words we generated in class today. If the word on the left has a root word, write it in the right-hand column.

Lesson 1—20 minutes	Lesson 2—20 minutes	Lesson 3—20 minutes
Week 1 Nifty Thrifty Intro:		
Week 2		
Week 3 Word Wall Words Intro:		
Week 4		

Other Choices:

Nifty Thrifty Word Cards Words Sorts Guess the Covered Word

Scavenger Hunt Word Detectives Making Words

What Looks Right?

Review Activities:

Be a Mind Reader Mini-WORDO Riddles

Month:

	Lesson 1—20 minutes	Lesson 2—20 minutes	Lesson 3—20 minutes
Week 1	Nifty Thrifty Intro: beautiful, classify, prettier, happiness, electricity, community, communities (pg. 51)	What Looks Right (pg. 61) Pattern: aid/ayed/ade	Word Sort -ly words (pg. 39 for directions)
Week 2	Nifty Thrifty Cards (pg. 24 for directions) Send homework to have them make new words and neologism	Guess the Covered Word Pull an excerpt from a favorite author	Making Words: secret word electrician (pg. 58)
Week 3	Word Wall Words Intro: they're, their, there, about, every, people, know, no, probably, enough	Scavenger Hunt for words ending with -ful (pg. 42 for directions)	Word Detectives content-area word: equation
Week 4	Be a Mind Reader with Word Wall words	Prefix Sort lesson im-	Mini-WORDO hopeless, impossible, richest, classify, happiness, electricity, beautiful, prettier, musician

Other Choices:

Nifty Thrifty Word Cards	Words Sorts	Guess the Covered Word
Scavenger Hunt	Word Detectives	Making Words

Review Activities:

Be a Mind Reader	Mini-WORDO	What Looks Right?	Riddles

Month:
November

Dear Parent,

Your child is participating in Balanced Literacy lessons from the Big-Blocks® Literacy Framework. In a Big-Blocks classroom, students are taught reading comprehension, how to select and enjoy a good book, writing skills and strategies, and how to read, spell, and understand words and develop vocabulary. Students spend approximately one hour per week Working with Words.

Students spend the majority of their time in the Working with Words Block looking at and studying big words—words with prefixes and suffixes. Learning strategies to help them read and understand big words is very important for upper-grade readers. While they are learning about big words, there are some small, common words they also need to learn to spell accurately. Approximately 100 words make up 50 percent of what the average writer, student or adult, writes on a daily basis. These words also make up the list of words students most often misspell. These frequently misspelled words are often practiced for short periods of time in the early grades but they are not studied long enough for students to learn them well. Since these words are the most often written words, the emphasis of spelling in a Big-Blocks classroom will be making sure students have time and opportunity to learn to spell these words accurately in all of their written work.

Teachers will review student writing to identify which words students need to practice. Once a set of frequently written and often misspelled words are identified, they will be placed on the Word Wall and will be reviewed regularly. Students will be expected to write these words correctly in all of their writing in all subject areas—all day, every day! Your child's grade will reflect how well he or she is spelling these words in the context of the real writing done each day in class.

For your information, a list of words will be sent home monthly. Any words being introduced that month are marked and all other words will continue to appear on the list. Please help your child learn to spell this very important list of words.

Sincerely,

Fifth Grade Teacher

References

Children's Works Cited

Alexander, Who Used to Be Rich Last Sunday by Judith Viorst (Scholastic, 1978)

Bats by Lisa deMauro (Parachute Press, Inc., 1990)

Book review of *Boy, http://search.barnesandnoble.com/booksearch/isbninquiry.asp?z=y&pwb=1&ean=9780141303055*

Boy: Tales of Childhood by Roald Dahl (Puffin, 1999)

Earthquakes by Deborah Heiligman (Scholastic Reference, 2003)

Everything You Need to Know About Science Homework by Anne Zeman and Kate Kelly (Scholastic Reference, 2005)

Freedom Train: The Story of Harriet Tubman by Dorothy Sterling (Scholastic, 1987)

Harcourt Horizons: United States History: Beginnings (Harcourt, 2005)

Heaven by Angela Johnson (Simon Pulse, 2000)

Lightning by Seymour Simon (HarperTrophy, 1999)

The Lucky Stone by Lucille Clifton (Yearling, 1986)

Molly McGinty Has a Really Good Day by Gary Paulsen (Yearling, 2006)

"Molly Pitcher" adapted from the Web site: *http://russell.gresham.k12.or.us/Colonial_America/Molly_Pitcher.html*.

Monkeying Around by Jane Hammerslough (Scholastic Paperbacks, 2003)

Movie review of *Shaggy Dog* excerpted from the Web site: *http://www.usatoday.com/life/movies/reviews/2006-03-09-shaggy-dog_x.htm*.

Mr. Lincoln's Way by Patricia Polacco (Scholastic, 2003)

Now Let Me Fly: The Story of a Slave Family by Dolores Johnson (Sagebrush, 1999)

Parasitic Life by Sam Brelsfoard (Pearson Education, Inc., 2006)

Punctuation Takes a Vacation by Robin Pulver (Holiday House, 2004)

The Revolutionary War by Brendan January (Children's Press, 2001)

The Sweetest Fig by Chris Van Allsburg (Houghton Mifflin, 1993)

A Three-Minute Speech: Lincoln's Remarks at Gettysburg by Jennifer Armstrong (Aladdin, 2003)

The Time Warp Trio: Your Mother Was a Neanderthal by Jon Scieszka (Puffin, 2004)

A Voice from the Border by Pamela Smith Hill (HarperTrophy, 2000)

Weather by Seymour Simon (HarperTrophy, 2000)

The Whipping Boy by Sid Fleischman (Greenwillow, 1986)

World War II for Kids: A History with 21 Activities by Richard Panchyk (Chicago Review Press, 2002)

Professional References

Arens, A. B., Loman, K. L., Cunningham, P. M., and Hall, D. P. (2005). *The Teacher's Guide to Big Blocks™: A Multimethod, Multilevel Framework*. Greensboro, NC: Carson-Dellosa Publishing Company.

Baumann, J. F., Edwards, E. C., Font, G., Tereshinski, C. A., Kame'enui, E. J., and Olejnik, S. (2002). "Teaching Morphemic and Contextual Analysis to Fifth-Grade Students." *Reading Research Quarterly*, 37, 150–176.

References

Carlisle, J. F., and Stone, C. A. (2005). "Exploring the Role of Morphemes in Word Reading." *Reading Research Quarterly*, 40, 428–449.

Cunningham, P. M. (2004). *Phonics They Use: Words for Reading and Writing* (4th edition). New York: Allyn & Bacon.

Cunningham, P. M. (1999). *Phonics They Use: Words for Reading and Writing* (3rd edition). New York: Allyn & Bacon.

Cunningham, P. M. (2002). *Prefixes and Suffixes: Systematic Sequential Phonics and Spelling*. Greensboro, NC: Carson-Dellosa Publishing Company.

Cunningham, P. M. (2000). *Systematic Sequential Phonics They Use*. Greensboro, NC: Carson-Dellosa Publishing Company.

Cunningham, P. M. (2004). *WordMaker*. Volo, IL: Don Johnston, Inc.

Cunningham, P. M. and Hall, D. P. (1994). *Making Big Words: Multilevel, Hands-on Spelling and Phonics Activities*. Parsippany, NJ: Good Apple.

Cunningham, P. M. (1997). *Making More Big Words*. Parsippany, NJ: Good Apple.

Cunningham, P. M. and Hall, D. P. (1998). *Month-by-Month Phonics for Upper Grades: A Second Chance for Struggling Readers and Students Learning English*. Greensboro, NC: Carson-Dellosa Publishing Company.

Cunningham, P. M. and Hall, D. P. (2005). *Reading/Writing Complex Rhymes: Rhymes With More Than One Spelling Pattern*. Greensboro, NC: Carson-Dellosa Publishing Company.

Cunningham, P. M. and Hall, D. P. (2005). *Reading/Writing Simple Rhymes: Simple Rhymes With One Spelling Pattern*. Greensboro, NC: Carson-Dellosa Publishing Company.

Cunningham, P. M., Hall, D. P., and Defee, M. (1998). "Nonability-Grouped, Multilevel Instruction: Eight Years Later." *The Reading Teacher*, 51, 652–664.

Dale, E. and O'Rourke, J. (1981). *The Living Word Vocabulary: A National Vocabulary Inventory*. Chicago: World Book-Childcraft International.

Fry, E. B., Polk, J. K., and Fountoukidis, D. (1985) *The Reading Teacher's Book of Lists*. Upper Saddle River, NJ: Prentice Hall.

Ivey, G., and Broaddus, K. (2000). "Tailoring the Fit: Reading Instruction and Middle School Readers." *The Reading Teacher*, 54, 68–78.

Nagy, W. and Anderson, R. C. (1984). "How Many Words Are There in Printed School English?" *Reading Research Quarterly*, 19, 304–330.

Nagy, W. E., Anderson, R. C., Schommer, M., Scott, J. A., and Stallman, A. C. (1989). "Morphological Families and Word Recognition." *Reading Research Quarterly*, 24, 262–282.

Donahue, P., Daane, M., and Grigg, W. (2003). *The Nation's Report Card: Reading Highlights 2003*. Washington, D.C.: U.S. Department of Education.

Stahl, S. A., Duffy-Hester, A. M., and Stahl, K. (1998). "Everything You Wanted to Know about Phonics (but Were Afraid to Ask)." *Reading Research Quarterly*, 33, 338–355.